The
Mister
Rogers
Effect

The
Mister
Rogers
Effect

7 Secrets to Bringing Out the Best
in Yourself and Others
from America's Beloved Neighbor

DR. ANITA KNIGHT KUHNLEY

BakerBooks
a division of Baker Publishing Group
Grand Rapids, Michigan

© 2020 by Anita Knight Kuhnley

Published by Baker Books
a division of Baker Publishing Group
PO Box 6287, Grand Rapids, MI 49516-6287
www.bakerbooks.com

Printed in the United States of America

Library of Congress Cataloging-in-Publication Data
Names: Kuhnley, Anita Knight, 1980– author.
Title: The Mister Rogers effect : 7 secrets to bringing out the best in yourself and
.   others from America's beloved neighbor / Anita Knight Kuhnley.
Description: Grand Rapids : Baker Books, 2020.
Identifiers: LCCN 2020008738 | ISBN 9781540900296 (paperback)
Subjects: LCSH: Mister Rogers neighborhood (Television program) | Conduct of
   life. | Rogers, Fred—Influence.
Classification: LCC PN1992.4.R56 K84 2020 | DDC 791.45/72—dc23
LC record available at https://lccn.loc.gov/2020008738

ISBN 978-1-5409-0113-2 (hardcover)

The author is represented by Hartline Literary Agency.

20   21   22   23   24   25   26   7   6   5   4   3   2

In loving memory of my Mims—
my grandmother.

She was also known as Dr. Ida Molina-Zinam.
She consistently brought out the best in herself
and others. At ninety-one years young,
Mims died during the preparation
of this manuscript, but her last prayer
with me was for the readers of this book
and for the positive effect that it
would have on them. Thank you for helping
me honor her memory.

Contents

Part 1

Mister Rogers

A World without Mister Rogers

Many have said, "We need a Mr. Rogers in our world today." I believe that if you can't find a Mr. Rogers, you can certainly be one. Internalize his message and be a healing, calming presence. I fail miserably, but I'm trying.

comment on YouTube video "Remembering
Mr. Rogers," a video interview with
Charlie Rose, televised in 1994

I will never forget the day I had a discussion with my students that would send me on a transformative quest. It was quiet in the large, dark classroom filled with aspiring counselors. I flipped on the fluorescent lights and looked out into the sea of faces. The powerful video clip had ended, and there were a few moments of contemplative silence before sniffles could be heard and tear-filled eyes met mine. After pausing for a moment, I asked, "What was it like for you to watch this video of Mister Rogers advocating for public television, addressing Senator Pastore, and talking about how to address anger?"

One student raised her hand. With sadness in her voice, she said, "I work in inner-city schools where we see children from all sorts of backgrounds, like single-parent homes, poverty, immigration. The kids I work with don't have a Mister Rogers. They have no one to teach them how to regulate their emotions, so they turn to violence. When they get angry, they fight." This was the beginning of a lively discussion.

That evening, while taking my dogs for a walk, I remembered my student's words: "They have no one." Some children have no safe adult to talk to; they have the sense that no one cares. They fall victim to an adult with no knowledge of how to regulate their own anger, then consequently turn to violence, grow up, and in turn hurt their own children. As kids, they likely longed for an escape from the violence, for someone to rescue them from people who did not know what to do with their anger—until they, too, adopted their parents' ways for lack of an alternative.

I knew I had to do something. I set out on a quest to uncover the psychological principles that Rogers used to transform Senator Pastore from his hostile and angry state of mind to a collaborative, friendly, even admiring ally. Mister Rogers skirted past Pastore's defenses to his vulnerable inner child and engaged in authentic connection (we work at unraveling this mystery in more detail in secret 2).

Rogers offered an alternative—something delightfully incongruent with the path of least resistance. What he offered was hope of a safe world for the young child in all of us and for our children and all the children of tomorrow. Compelled by something beyond myself, I knew I had to use the research tools that I had acquired through my training and the lens of psychology to unpack the mysterious principles that characterized his life and work. I set out to learn all that Mister Rogers embodied and generously offered to those around him. These findings became the source material I used to unravel the top seven psychological principles Rogers used to make a difference—lest my students and other adults continue to believe there is no hope for future generations.

Armed with my background in qualitative research, a panel of psychological experts, my own psychological training, and my tools—psychological principles, writing, and storytelling—I set out to identify and share the hope that comes with a step-by-step plan that we, Mister Rogers's television neighbors, can use to build a strong tower and refuge to

> *What he offered was hope of a safe world for the young child in all of us and for our children and all the children of tomorrow.*

protect the children (and the inner child in all of us). My work begs them not to believe the lie and reveals that there *is* an alternative; they can work through their anger because there is hope, and there are caring adults who will help them. This theme was one of the most salient concepts that emerged from Mister Rogers's work.

Mister Rogers Spoke to the Neglected and Lonely in Us

Mister Rogers spoke to the neglected inside all of us—the part of us that believes we need to work hard to earn any inkling of love in this world, that believes "just maybe if I can work hard enough, produce enough, or be good enough at something, then someone will love me." He reached straight past the expert striver, worker, and producer into a place deep inside of us. He cared deeply for his viewers, or television neighbors as he often referred to us, and he communicated this in every program, wherever he was, and whomever he was with.

His song "It's You I Like" is a radical message of acceptance and care, and he sang it often, sometimes personalizing the lyrics. When he appeared with comedian Joan Rivers, he improvised the words to match her personality: "It's you I like, it's not your jokes." And for a young Jeffrey Erlanger, who used a wheelchair, he threw in, "It's not your fancy chair." Jeffrey and Joan, from such different walks of life, each appeared awestruck for a moment, shocked with such surprise and wonder that they didn't know what to do. Joan Rivers pulled up Rogers's cardigan sweater, which she had been wearing, around her head and hid for a moment. Then she quickly removed it and smiled at Rogers as he continued singing straight to her heart.[1] Similarly, Jeffrey basked in his moment and giggled and smiled at Mister Rogers.[2]

It is as if Rogers knew that simply becoming familiar with someone was shallow water; instead he always pursued the deep dive. He was not satisfied with small talk or just knowing what was on the outside; he pursued true knowing and intimacy with everyone he met.

Rogers could reach the inner orphan, the lost and lonely, the down and out or the high and mighty. It did not really matter who was in front of him—he wanted to search for the good in that person. Perhaps the day he was bullied as a child for his outer appearance was the day he developed new eyes to search for the best in his neighbors and to truly know them. This was demonstrated over and over in his interactions with others both privately and publicly. He started each show by inviting his viewers to belong, to be his neighbors, and he ended each show with expressions of care.

Finding a Safe Haven—Even on Television

Mister Rogers was moved by demeaning behavior; he could not bear to see one human being degraded or humiliated by another. It made him angry, and he wanted to do something about it. Rogers told his journalist friend Amy Hollingsworth in their first interview, "I got into television because I saw people throwing pies at each other's faces, and that to me was such demeaning behavior. And if there's anything that bothers me, it's one person demeaning another. That really makes me mad!"[3]

"How can we make goodness attractive?" he wondered. "And how can we encourage quiet reflection rather than noise?"[4] In a world that was sedated by the lullaby of noisy television, Rogers was awake to the knowledge that there was something of virtue in this powerful medium.

This was revolutionary thinking in the early years of television. Fred Rogers raised the bar for quality in children's television production. He understood that there were children who felt alone in the world and had no safe place to go. He created that haven of safety on his show, giving viewers a pocket of time to watch someone who communicated care for them, who communicated that their feelings were safe with him, and who was there for them.

Before Mister Rogers came along, the slapstick, pie-in-your-face–style comedy abounded on television. But the difference Rogers offered was meaningful. He'd studied child psychology in college, forming a close relationship with one of his professors, Dr. Margaret McFarland, a child psychologist.[5] Dr. McFarland mentored him for thirty years. Rogers also had the opportunity to hear Anna Freud, an expert in child psychology, known as a child analyst, and the youngest daughter of Sigmund Freud, when she offered a new perspective on a psychological case.[6] Instead of encouraging her audience to study what was wrong about the case or perform the usual analysis of the diagnosis and problems, which is commonplace in clinical circles, she presented a question that fascinated Rogers. Anna Freud encouraged her listeners to examine how someone could go through so much difficulty and still overcome it and thrive.[7]

Rogers also wanted to have eyes that searched for the strengths in others and called them forth to shine. He seemed to have the capacity to transform people in very short interactions, helping them feel safe and comforted.

Why We Move Toward or Away from Relationship

Felt safety is foundational for secure relationships. Mister Rogers understood the importance of this principle and was versed in child psychology and development courtesy of his mentor and guide, Dr. McFarland, whom he credited as "the most major influence on [his] professional life."[8] One of the most prominent theories of psychological development is called attachment theory.

Children who are neglected do not have an attachment figure, a safe person whom they can count on to be responsive and always be there for them. These children may go through many different caregivers in the early years of life due to high turnover. This is difficult for a child's physiological attachment system. *Attachment* is a word that will come up throughout this text. Attachment theory—sometimes called *relationship theory*—describes the nature of the bond between a child and his or her caregiver. A child's ability to attach often predicts the state of mind a child will have toward relationships later in life.

Imagine this scenario. A mother sits her baby down in the nursery to play while she and friendly researchers observe. The baby plays with toys spread out on the floor, making eye contact with Mom, who smiles and nods back. The baby resumes playing, then Mom gets up and slips out of the room. The baby is noticeably upset; she cries. One of the researchers sits on the floor, trying to interest the child in a toy, and is eventually successful. Still, the baby is tearful, and she glances back toward the door eagerly awaiting Mom's return.

A few minutes later, Mom returns, and the baby quickly begins crawling toward her. At last, the crying has ceased! Mom picks baby up right away, and after the two hug, the baby quickly calms and is ready for play again. This is the essence of secure attachment style—also known as relationship style—in action!

One of the main purposes of the attachment system is to seek closeness to a caregiver. In order to survive, a baby must stay close to a parent or caregiver in order to get the care he or she needs. A parent provides nourishment for a child's biological needs but also for the child's emotional and psychological needs in most cases. The child goes to the parent for comfort, soothing, food, diaper changes, and help calming their feelings of distress. Seeking closeness to a parent during childhood—or a relationship partner such as a spouse or a special close friend during adulthood—can be calming and soothing. This relationship where the parent serves as a safe haven during times of distress and a secure base from which the child can launch and explore the world is the ideal outcome.

However, what happens in cases where a child does not have a caregiver they can count on, on a regular and relatively consistent basis? There are four different outcomes (or attachment styles) that typically develop. Three of the four styles are organized (secure, preoccupied, and dismissing), meaning that the child has a predictable strategy of relating to others. The fourth is more chaotic and does not have a predictable organizational pattern. These are the four approaches to relationship:

1. **Secure attachment style**—an organized style characterized by a sense of safety in relationships and the belief that the self is lovable and others are competent to show love.

2. **Preoccupied attachment style**—an organized style characterized by a sense of anxiety with a tendency to get dysfunctionally tangled up in relationships. This style is also characterized by the belief that the self is not worthy of love, but others are competent to love.

3. **Dismissing attachment style**—an organized style characterized by a sense of aloofness or a pushing away of attachment relationships. There is often

a history of rejection and a belief that the self is worthy of love, but others are not competent to show love.

4. **Unresolved for loss or Unresolved for abuse**—a disorganized style characterized by the belief that the self is not worthy of love and others are not able to love: "The grass is dead on both sides of the fence." It often stems from a history of loss or abuse.[9]

Let's explore an example of one of these relational styles in action, the dismissing style. In one scenario, a child may experience rejection. Perhaps a parent is busy due to overwork, is struggling with depression, or is otherwise occupied. This parent then tells the child when the child approaches, "Go play in your room," "Go play with your siblings," "Go do the dishes," "Go outside," or even, "Go away." Any iteration of "Get out of here" sends the child an important message. In essence, if the parent *pushes the child away*, the child experiences rejection.

It is important to remember that doing this now and then is unlikely to be problematic. There is some of this in all attachment style histories, even for those that are securely attached. However, when this becomes the pervasive interaction style of the parent, the child is likely to develop a dismissing style of relating to others.

Early experiences leave a stamp on us; though it may not be seen with the eyes, it is there.[10] This rejection leaves children with the idea that they cannot go to other people in times of distress; the underlying belief is that others won't be able to help. Also, by going to a rejecting parent during times of distress, the child may risk alienating the parent further. So the child will often turn away from the parent and turn inward or turn toward objects.

After repeated experiences of rejection, children who have learned the dismissing attachment style can learn to mask their emotions and sense of needing and wanting closeness to their caregivers *as early as three years old*. These children do not cry when seeing their parents leave them alone in a nursery. Their play slows, and when the parent returns, they do not go to the parent. Instead, their play picks back up. This may be deceiving since they do not appear distressed—though they still experience the physiological markers of distress. Heart rate and blood pressure may increase, just like in the kids who are screaming their heads off and crawling after their parents. They mask these feelings for survival. Like a duck flailing its legs under the water but appearing to smoothly sail across the lake, these children experience inner tumult but appear unfazed on the surface.

Children who exhibit the dismissing attachment style may also learn to dismiss their own feelings, as well as other relationships, and turn toward things. Some of my clients with this style of attachment may have elaborate collections and be oriented toward things rather than people. They are sometimes thought of by peers and family members as a "lone wolf." There are several other insecure styles that can develop with repeated experiences in relationships that communicate in one way or another, "Your feelings are not important. Other people matter more than you. Reaching out to others or being vulnerable will earn you nothing but hurt or rejection." It is beyond the scope of this text to explore in detail each style.[11] Insecure relational patterns develop in response to rejection to keep a child safe from the crudeness of these realities in their early relationships.

Mister Rogers Offered the Hope of a Different World

Fred Rogers presented something that made the difficulties of reality easier to bear. He countered the myths that children often hear. Maybe you were told that children are to be seen and not heard, meaning what you have to say, think, or feel does not really matter. This, and messages like it, communicate that feelings do not matter unless they are positive.

Though Mister Rogers is no longer with us, there is a bit of him in all of us who grew up with the neighborhood.

In a world asleep to the treasures of children, and our own inner child, Mister Rogers gently roused us to wakefulness through his culturally incongruent messages: He taught us that it is okay to talk about feelings, even unpleasant ones. He taught that children matter, and the inner child in all of us is important to nurture. He taught that feelings are both mentionable and manageable. These and other important healing messages often allowed him to have a transformative effect on his neighbors in just minutes. Even though Mister Rogers is no longer with us, there is a bit of him in all of us who grew with the neighborhood. We have the ability to keep the love and care he shared with us alive so the world never has to know a world without Rogers's legacy. In the pages to come, we will explore some key strategies to do just that.

The Quest for Mister Rogers's Secrets

I grew up watching *Mister Rogers' Neighborhood* on TV, and I remember Mister Rogers's gentle voice and kind eyes. I remember hearing him sing about the beautiful day in the neighborhood or what to do with the mad that you feel. I *learned* from Mister Rogers. As an adult, I thought the messages he put into the world need to be made accessible to anyone who wants to learn more about how to have such an influence. But how could we learn key principles from Rogers, small ways to make a big difference for ourselves and those around us?

I was inspired by my students and the thought of the neglected, the lonely, and the orphaned. I was inspired by what Mister Rogers had to teach all of us. The task set before me was important: to uncover these key principles, write about Rogers's work, and help parents, grandparents, counselors, coaches, teachers, and others keep his influence alive! Our feelings are mentionable and manageable, and people do not have to turn to violence because their anger is out of control, or to suicide because their pain is unrelenting. Mister Rogers firmly believed that by helping people learn how to manage painful feelings like anger and sadness, we could make their tomorrows safer.

This idea of managing emotions prompted me to search my memory for incidents where I experienced children (of all ages) who were unable to regulate their anger. Unfortunately, I had plenty of these memories. For example, I recalled working at a substance abuse rehabilitation facility for adolescent males. Each young man at the facility had turned to drugs and alcohol and other destructive behaviors (such as maxing out Mom's credit card on thirty thousand dollars' worth of virtual equipment for video games like World of Warcraft) as a short-term way to numb the pain, emptiness, anger, and loneliness in their lives. After thinking through these examples, I asked myself, what if we could go back to Mister Rogers's lessons and learn a new way to deal with our emotions? A way that would help us not only address our feelings but achieve even more authentic connection and intimacy because of our painful feelings? A way to cultivate gratitude as a lifestyle?

These are some of the questions I studied, and the answers I found may surprise you. They are contained within the seven key principles in this text. Although the psychological principles informing his work were not limited to these seven secrets alone, this book explores seven of the keys that emerged as themes throughout his work.

1. Listen First

2. Validate Feelings

3. Pause and Think

4. Show Gratitude

5. Develop Empathy

6. Practice Acceptance

7. Establish Security

Mister Rogers also valued inquiry and wonder, so in honor of the inquisitive man, there is a brief concept at the end of each chapter that invites you to reflect on what you've learned, which as Rogers would say "is really more important than all the text."[12] These sections, which are designed to nourish the appetite of the hungry soul while also leaving a hunger for more, are called "A Concept to Contemplate."

Consider this an escape from all the noise that threatens the destruction of the imagination and an invitation to one of the highest expressions of the human spirit: making a difference by being who you really are. Mister Rogers invited us to be who we really are; he invited us to be our best selves with his unwavering gaze on what was good in everyone he met. His lessons continue to beckon us to take a peek at our neighbors through this lens of kindness and let the darkness disappear into a flash of light.

> *Mister Rogers invited us to be our best selves with his unwavering gaze on what was good in everyone he met.*

Rub It In

When I was growing up as an oldest child of four, it was often incumbent upon me to take care of my younger siblings. A bright spot on many days was my baby brother's humor. You see, Paul had very kissable cheeks as babies often do, and I would kiss them often. One day when he was about four, after I had given him some kisses, I saw him rubbing his cheek. I said, "Aw, Paul, are you wiping off my kisses?" He looked at me with great sincerity, his eyes wide as he responded, "I am not wiping them off, I am rubbing them in!"

I smile every time I think of that memory! Paul does not share my love for that story, but he gave me permission to tell it—but not without reminding me it is important to make sure kisses are not wet or slobbery, as one would expect nothing less from a baby brother turned adult. His incredible emotional intelligence, insight, and sweet words from that moment continue to nourish my heart. When I find something I admire in someone, I often let them know I hope they rub off on me. But in the words of my brother, I would like to rub Mister Rogers *in* to my soul. I would like more of what he offered the world in me and those I meet. This book is an invitation to, as Paul might say, *rub it in.* To embrace questions as they are: invitations to wonder rather than be consumed. Mister Rogers beckons us to savor and enjoy questions rather than just pursue answers. As the poet Rainer Maria Rilke said,

> Be patient toward all that is unsolved in your heart and try to love the questions themselves. . . . Live the questions now. Perhaps you will then gradually, without noticing it, live along some distant day into the answer.[13]

There will never be anyone just like Mister Rogers. He wanted each of us to remember that there is no one else in the world like you or me; we are all one of a kind. In remembering what Mister Rogers taught us, we can keep a bit of the love and expressions of care he shared with us by paying them forward. The principles and concepts to contemplate are at times heartwarming and at other times unsettling as they invite us to journey toward a depth of knowing and being known. So, neighbor, enjoy the journey along the path of keeping Mister Rogers's legacy alive in our neighborhoods!

A CONCEPT TO CONTEMPLATE

Mister Rogers had a way of transforming everyone he met into a neighbor—a treasured friend. He used authentic care, demonstrated in part by seven secrets—careful listening, validation of emotions, reflection, gratitude, empathy, acceptance, and expressions of care—to form lasting, loving relationships with people of all ages. You can too.

The Mister Rogers Effect

It helps to be loved in order to work in this life.

Fred Rogers, in an interview with
Charlie Rose on PBS, 1994

*T*n 1981 a ten-year-old boy rolled onto a television set
in his electric wheelchair, expertly maneuvering it into
a television neighborhood and into America's living rooms.

Meanwhile, a young Mister Rogers—dressed in a tie and
cardigan, dark hair neatly parted—stepped outside his television home and enthusiastically welcomed the boy, seated
himself at eye level, and admired the boy's wheelchair, saying, "That's a very fancy machine!" He paused to acknowledge the boy's expertise in operating it: "but *you're* the one
who makes it go." Then he asked, "Did it take you a long
time to learn to operate the machine?"

The boy's name was Jeffrey Erlanger, and he enthusiastically told Mister Rogers it only took him one day to learn
the chair. A wider smile spread across Mister Rogers's face

as he leaned in. "How proud your parents must be!" Jeff shone, smiling and nodding.

Now that Mister Rogers had expressed appreciation for Jeff's abilities and seen the best in him, the boy was feeling loved, secure, and ready to explore. Thus Mister Rogers ventured to a new topic. There was, after all, the elephant in the room. Rogers's unwavering gaze was fixed on what was good in Jeff.

That day, Mister Rogers forsook the superficial and pursued true knowing; he began a dialogue with Jeffrey on national television, asking him if he would reveal to their television neighbors what happened that made him need the wheelchair. Jeff cheerfully agreed, explaining that when he was about seven months old, he had a tumor that "broke the nerves" that send the signals for movement to his hands and legs. Jeff said, "They tried to cut the tumor, but they couldn't get it, and I became handicapped, and I got a wheelchair when I was four years old." With a concerned but peaceful expression, Mister Rogers asked if Jeff remembered this, and the boy said he did. Rogers went on to express appreciation for Jeff's doctors: "You must have some mighty good doctors that are taking care of you! Can you tell me any of your doctors' names?" Jeff listed their names and their different specialties.

Mister Rogers forsook the superficial and pursued true knowing.

Rogers continued his discussion with expressions of care and awe as Jeffrey revealed the details of a recent stomach problem. All across America, children moved closer to their television sets, interested in understanding what all this meant. Jeffrey explained, "I had surgery this summer because I have a pain in my stomach called autonomic dysreflexia." Mister Rogers, impressed and fascinated, asked Jeff to repeat these big words. With a grin spreading across his face, the boy carefully enunciated *auto-nomic dys-reflex-ia*. Though he confessed that he was not exactly sure what it meant—Mister Rogers cut in and proudly exclaimed, "But you sure can say it!" The bond and fondness each had toward the other was visible. As their chat progressed, Rogers noted that Jeff was able to speak about these things well, and he suggested that Jeff might be able to help other people who have similar struggles.

Every time I watch this episode, I can feel the sense of intimacy and connection between Rogers and Erlanger, but the beauty of the moment did not stop there. Rogers's relentless pursuit of connection provoked another invitation—to sing together. The song they performed is called "It's You I Like," and it's about liking a person for who he or she is inside, not because of their outward appearance or anything external. Rogers sings, "It's you I like . . . the way down deep inside you." He even personalized the song to Jeffrey, as I mentioned earlier, and emphasized that liking him did not involve his material items, such as his wheelchair.

After they sang together, Rogers changed the subject, a thoughtful and interested look spreading across his face. He explored feelings with Jeff. Specifically, he wanted to know about Jeff's sad feelings. Rogers, with a look of great care and concern, leaned toward Jeff and began again.

Rogers was not afraid to talk about painful or difficult things. With a knowing expression, as if to understand some of the sadness that must be inherent in facing autonomic dysreflexia as a young child, the inquisitive Rogers plunged deeper with a most important question, "What do you do when you are feeling blue?" Rogers normalized this feeling as he talked about it in such a knowing way. Jeff's answer was that it depended. Rogers offered suggestions and asked if Jeff did things like make up stories. Rogers confessed that he had done those things himself. Jeff broke in, taken with this and captivated by wonder, by asking if making up stories helped Rogers.[1]

The magic—the "Mister Rogers Effect"—had happened. It was as if Rogers's attitude had been caught.

Time Passes but Some Things Stay the Same

Nearly two decades passed after Jeff and Mister Rogers's first encounter. If we fast-forward to 1999, when a much older Fred Rogers sat in his tuxedo in the audience for the Television Hall of Fame induction ceremony, we see that darkness quickly turned to light onstage, revealing an older Jeffrey Erlanger once again skillfully maneuvering his fancy electric wheelchair. Rogers's jaw dropped as he leapt from his seat, immediately recognizing his friend. The years had not dampened his enthusiasm nor his expression of care. He ran to Jeffrey, arms open, and embraced him, sharing how happy he was to see him. Over the resounding applause, Jeffrey debunked any suspicion that Rogers was anything but sincere for all of America to hear as he declared,

> It is an honor to be here tonight to be a part of your proud moment. When you tell people "it is you I like," we know

that you really mean it. And tonight, I want to let you know on behalf of millions of children and grown-ups, it is *you* that I like.[2]

The response? The two were rewarded with a roar of applause and a standing ovation. The applause declared appreciation for Mister Rogers himself and vanquished any question of his relevance. The first television interaction Rogers had with the young Erlanger was only about ten minutes long, and yet those ten minutes deeply impacted both of their lives. It appeared that Mister Rogers's expression of his belief in and admiration for Erlanger and the words he spoke to him emphasized his capacity to help others with similar problems. This impact stayed with Erlanger, so much so that he made it a point to be there for his friend at the sunset of Rogers's career.

The Mister Rogers Effect

Jeffrey Erlanger and Fred Rogers are no longer with us.[3] However, the effect that Mister Rogers had on our world can be carried forward. I recently met a young college student in the library who saw that my research team and I were working on a Mister Rogers project, and he told us that he had watched Mister Rogers the previous night on YouTube. He said the show helped him relax so he could fall asleep—he loved the calming effect Mister Rogers had on him.

So what is this healing effect that Rogers had on America, which is still influencing us more than a decade after losing our beloved neighbor. What is the effect that left his television neighbors' eyes welling with tears and hearts swelling with the sense of connection to their loved ones? How did Rogers keep both America's children and their parents coming back to watch his show years later? Psychological literature and the problems that bring people into counseling reveal some answers. Because many of us have experienced neglect and difficulty managing feelings like anger and sadness, we are unprepared to develop into healthy, secure neighbors. Mister Rogers understood this and invited the most vulnerable parts within his audience members to receive his neighborly expressions of care. He connected with neighbors in real, authentic ways.

Throughout these pages we will explore Mister Rogers's recipe with the key psychological ingredients he used to have this effect. Consider some of the comments from people who viewed his visit to *The Rosie O'Donnell Show*, where Rogers brought her a seashell and introduced his puppets King Friday and Daniel Tiger. Notice that although he has been gone for many years, people sometimes talk about him like they just encountered him in the flesh this morning:

I think Mister Rogers was a real-life angel.[4]

He's not even speaking yet, and I agree with him.[5]

The heartbeat behind *The Mister Rogers Effect*, represented by a dialogue between viewers missing Mister Rogers and consoling one another so we can keep his legacy alive, is summed up with this statement:

As long as people like us keep his message, his teaching and his memory sacred, he will always be here. . . . I just wish I could have had the chance to thank him in person.[6]

Clearly Mister Rogers is missed. He had a calming effect on many. I also wish I could have met him while he was still here. He knew that we are all worthy of love and value, and he connected with people from all different backgrounds. One viewer said, "Yo no white man will never have a place in my heart like Mister Rogers."[7]

Regarding Rogers's impact on racial relations, another viewer said,

Mr. Rogers witnessed a period in history before black people and women were allowed to have basic rights in America. It's part of the reason why he had Officer Clemmons on the program, to show America that black people are just as kind, loving, and deserving of love as anyone else.[8]

Mister Rogers modeled the importance of embracing people from all racial backgrounds and demonstrated he cared for all of his neighbors. In a world polarized by religion and politics, it was clear Mister Rogers impacted, deeply cared for, and was in return loved by people of diverse backgrounds. He connected with people from all walks of life.

> *He connected with people from all walks of life.*

Rogers was able to reach people whose religious backgrounds and beliefs were very different from his own (he was trained as a Presbyterian minister).

That is not an easy feat. He affected people in ways that touched something raw and universal in each of us. Some of his viewers remarked,

> This guy was like some American master of Zen—and he didn't even know it, he just was. I believe that in fact is the very definition of being a Buddha.[9]

> God had [come] down from heaven and walked among us in human form. His name was Fred McFeely Rogers.[10]

> I'm not religious, but I'd consider Mr. Rogers a "saint."[11]

Pass It On

In addition to missing Mister Rogers and expressing appreciation and love for him, his television neighbors often reflect on how much we need his kindness and the lessons he taught us now. Some viewers long for the man himself, his comforting voice and kind smile, sharing sentiments like "It's so rare that someone talks to children like real people. We need this man today." Others respond with encouragement to carry his lessons onward and express appreciation for his statement about how tears and sweat often bring out the best in us. Some fans challenged others to focus on the important lessons Mister Rogers taught us rather than on how to bring Fred Rogers himself back to life. We need to keep the lessons he taught in our hearts and pass them on to others.

This text is an effort to do just that, to identify the psychological principles that were prominent in his work and to adapt these seven "secrets" so we can carry on his legacy in every neighborhood.

Three-year-old Michael once wrote a letter to Mister Rogers about the death of his dog, Max, and the fact that he still felt sad. Mister Rogers responded with a kind and empathetic letter that included this thought: "Happy times and sad times are part of everyone's life, but you can grow to know that the love you and Max shared is still alive in you and always will be."[12]

Mister Rogers reminded us that just like sweat, tears are a part of life. Life comes with both happy and sad times. However, Rogers comforted Michael by confirming the special love he shared with Max would always be alive in Michael's heart. Death could not rob him of that. Likewise, Mister Rogers would have wanted his television neighbors to know that the care he shared for us, and the care we have for him, will always live on in our hearts. (This principle holds true for all of our loved ones. The love we have had for the loved ones we've lost and the love they had for us lives on in our hearts, even after their time on earth is through.) We can multiply the effect Rogers's expressions of care had on us as we share them with others.

> *We need to keep the lessons he taught in our hearts and pass them on to others.*

But how? I worked with a panel of psychological experts using qualitative research tools to analyze Rogers's work through a psychological lens and uncover seven key themes in his work, or what he sometimes called his offering of an expression of care.[13] The following pages share these psychological keys, examples of how Mister Rogers used them, and strategies to implement them in our own neighborhoods.

Mister Rogers's psychological techniques will soon not be mysterious secrets but practices any of us can use to effect change in ourselves, our families, our neighborhoods and, as Mister Rogers would say, in our own special ways.

A CONCEPT TO CONTEMPLATE

Mister Rogers always forsook the superficial and pursued true knowing. Good neighbors do. They care in authentic, genuine ways as they establish relationship. They are kind to people of all races, religions, and political persuasions. This is a good strategy for connecting with neighbors. What is one action you can take in order to better know your neighbors and loved ones and express kindness and appreciation for their differences?

Part 2

The Seven Secrets

Listen First

Listen with More than Your Ears

We speak with more than our mouths. We listen with more than our ears.

Fred Rogers, *Life's Journeys*
According to Mister Rogers

Some years ago I was at work in a university's counseling center when Jade, a young woman of about nineteen, entered with her professor Dr. Ham. Jade was crying quiet tears. The professor furrowed his thick brows and shifted his weight uncomfortably. Our office manager, who had been shuffling forms on her desk, glanced up at Jade. "How can I help you?" she asked. Jade squirmed, tears streaming down her pale cheeks, and mumbled something. Dr. Ham interrupted brusquely. "She would like to see a counselor right away about an incident."

With only cubicles for landing spots, we adopted empty classrooms for counseling. Jade accompanied me as I scouted for an open room. Spotting one, I placed a "Do Not Disturb" sign on the door, and in we went.

As we settled in, I asked her, "What brought you in for counseling?" Jade paused for a moment, and it seemed like the wheels in her head were turning quietly as she gazed upward. The large, musty classroom was quiet. I was quiet as well. Jade looked down and sniffled. As our eyes met, she choked, "Well, Dr. Ham was talking about sexual assault today, and I realized it happened to me. I couldn't stop crying, so after class he suggested counseling and offered to accompany me here."

I leaned forward, inviting her to continue. A friend of a friend had invited her over one evening the previous week. Things had not gone as planned. She said, "I went over just to hang out, thinking it would be cool. All of a sudden, he put his hands all over me. I said stop, but . . ."

Jade disclosed the details of the assault and her feelings of pain and loneliness, especially over the rebuttals she encountered when she attempted to talk to family about the trauma. When she tried to tell her story, she was met with either silence or blame for being promiscuous. The feelings of abandonment and pain rolled over her in waves. We spent time processing these experiences, and I sought to listen carefully and be present with her emotionally. This was even more critical, given the fact that she was courageously taking the first steps toward healing by telling her story in its fullness. As we continued our session, Jade expressed gratitude for the opportunity to share her experience for the *first* time, and I stood with her in the pain.

Later, when it came time to inquire about her goals for counseling, though, she became stuck.

I invited her to join me in a visualization exercise called the miracle question.[1] This question compels us to *imagine life without the problem*. It paints a picture of the desired outcome (or end goal) and outlines the path forward.

Tentatively—since this was early in our counseling relationship—I invited her to feel safe: "Would you feel comfortable if I asked you a question a bit out of the ordinary that requires some imagination?" Her eyes brightened with curiosity and she nodded.

"Okay," I said, "let's imagine that tonight you go home, put on your most comfy pajamas, and slip under the covers. You drift into a deep sleep. While you are dreaming, a miracle happens. Everything that was upsetting you is now resolved. Night turns to morning, and as the light seeps past the curtains, you awake. Tell me about what would be different about *you* when you woke up."

After taking some space to ponder, a scene emerged in Jade's mind's eye. "I would be in a locked room. In that room with me would be my mom, my dad, my sister, and my best friend, Adam. None of them would be allowed to leave until they heard everything I had to say!" she said with a hybrid of a laugh and a sigh. Jade wanted to be understood by the people she loved. She didn't want to be blamed, misunderstood, or overlooked. *Her miracle was to be heard by the people she loved.*

Listening to Hear and Understand

Jade is not alone in this. In fact, we all need to be truly heard and understood; this is the first of Mister Rogers's secrets.

He was an expert listener, and his humility made it clear that he was listening to understand and to know the other person—rather than to respond. Mister Rogers understood the role of listening in authentic connection.

To bring out the best in ourselves and others, then, we must learn *true listening*. It's something we do every day, but sometimes not in the right way. Often we listen to respond, to critique, or even to argue. However, the secret to making listening as therapeutic as the love of a doting grandparent is listening to understand. Rogers demonstrated this in numerous ways in his program, in his letters, and with his journalist friends.

But what is it that makes this process difficult and overrules our listening hearts? Sometimes good intentions get in the way of effective listening, like wanting to fix a problem or wanting to disclose one's own anecdotes. Sometimes our enthusiasm to share our own experience overrules our empathy, and we fail to listen well. Additionally, standing with a person in their pain—to really hear and see them even amidst suffering—can be uncomfortable, and we again fail at listening.

Here's an example from my classroom. As counselor trainees are learning active listening skills in class, they often ask me what is and isn't okay to say to a client. One student shared an example. "My client told me he stopped feeling as if life was happening to him and began to feel like an active participant in his life." The student asked, "So is it okay to say, 'Now can you see how this was the case all along?'"

In response, I reminded him, "Remember the litmus test for the listening skills is this—will what I say to my client help me seek to understand them, or help *me* to be understood?"

I paused and looked at him. "So does this help you understand him or help you to be understood?"

With a knowing smile he looked up and said, "Ah, okay, it helps me to be understood." Then he went on with the session with a more others-focused way of listening.

In order to listen well to our neighbors, we need to listen not only to hear with our ears but also with a desire to truly understand what it is like to see life through their eyes and experience it through their skin. We need to listen to understand what it is like to walk around in their world.

And being *heard* feels so similar to being *loved* that for many people the distinction goes unnoticed.[2] There is research evidence to suggest if two people at odds with one another take time to hear each other (for the purposes of understanding, not arguing), they develop a more favorable attitude toward the other. This phenomenon is true for not only acquaintances who disagree but romantic love as well.

An experiment was conducted by psychologist Arthur Aron, who invited pairs of strangers into a laboratory to ask one another thirty-six questions that would gradually create emotional closeness.[3] Famously, one couple fell in love. Of course, the inquisitive conversation partners also took time to listen to the answers that emerged. Through the process of listening to one another, the circuitous route to intimacy and connection became straighter.

> *Being* heard *feels so similar to being* loved *that for many people the distinction goes unnoticed.*

When training helpers in listening skills, counselor educators emphasize the physical posture of listening—but the posture of the heart is even more important. Even if you do all the right things in terms of skill and posture, if there is no care, concern, or desire to hear and understand the other person, then true listening is absent. As we have seen over and over in Mister Rogers's PBS television program, the posture of Rogers's heart was bent toward listening to understand his neighbors' hearts.

The Mister Rogers Effect: Feeling Heard and Feeling Loved

In the late 1980s, eight-year-old Beth Usher's phone rang, and an expert listener was on the line. Beth had a rare disease that caused her to have epileptic seizures, and she was facing a surgical procedure called a hemispherectomy that would remove half of her brain. Beth had been suffering from dozens of seizures a day that persisted for years, but *Mister Rogers' Neighborhood* provided such soothing that Beth ceased to have seizures while she watched the program. Her family contacted Mister Rogers's staff to tell them what a calming effect Mister Rogers's voice seemed to have.

And so he called. Mister Rogers greeted Beth with the same gentle voice that had reduced her seizures. Their conversation presents itself as a beautiful example of the thin line between feeling heard and feeling loved.

Beth confessed her fears and her desire for an end to the seizures to Mister Rogers. He listened. She admitted that she wanted her classmates to like her and play with her. He listened some more, hearing her soul's longing. She also revealed her fears of dying and leaving her beloved brother, things she had never spoken aloud before. He listened and spoke words of comfort to her, reminding Beth that her family and her doctors would take great care of her (see secret 7).

Beth and Mister Rogers's conversational intimacy lasted over an hour. The power of being heard had such an impact on Beth that she was seemingly lovestruck, as only an eight-year-old girl can be. Recall, too, we have noted that listening is a close relative to love. Overcome by Mister Rogers's expression of kindness as he took time to listen and care, her heart was gripped so powerfully by a sense of being understood that she was compelled to respond by verbalizing her love for Mister Rogers as they ended their conversation. Before they said their goodbyes, Beth said these important words: *"I love you, Mister Rogers."*

Mister Rogers responded in kind. How fitting that Beth was moved to express her love for her beloved neighbor who listened with both his ears and his heart! The prospect of a long and dangerous operation must have been so scary for this young girl—the dangers of prolonged sleep confront us even in childhood fantasy, such as tales of slumbering protagonists like Sleeping Beauty, who fell into a hundred-year sleep by pricking her finger on a spindle, or Dorothy from *The Wizard of Oz*, who was lulled into drowsiness by a field of poisonous poppies.

Like these classic stories, Beth's story had a happy ending. Mister Rogers, along with his puppets, also came to visit her in the hospital. Her surgery was successful. Despite being in a coma for a while, she awakened and healed from her surgery and lives to tell this beautiful story of her listening neighbor who was not afraid to talk with her about fears and hopes and who became her beloved friend for the rest of his life.[4]

The Psychology of Listening with More than Your Ears

Listening is often taken for granted in our 24/7 society. True listening takes practice and intentionality. We aren't born knowing how to listen well—we must learn because listening is considered the oldest and most important of the communication skills.[5]

Being heard by a receptive listener is a powerful experience. As one of my former students shared, it helps us to declutter our insides and consolidate our thinking. Being heard also helps us clarify our core feelings. When we divulge our story to a receptive listener, they use active listening skills like paraphrasing to help us become better narrators. When we hear our story in their words, we gain new insight. We can listen to ourselves better as we are listened to and heard by others.[6] Likewise, when we use empathetic and receptive listening to help others feel heard, we help them to obtain these same therapeutic effects.

We've seen what happens when speakers feel heard by a receptive listener. Sometimes they exclaim, "Yes! You get me!" Research suggests that when people feel heard, their attitude toward the listener can change from negative to positive.[7] Being heard has a powerful and distinct effect.

> *We can listen to ourselves better as we are listened to and heard by others.*

When someone experiences a lack of love in early childhood relationships, they might face deep-seated feelings of grief and loneliness that are not regulated or sorted through. Sometimes they develop unhealthy ways of coping with the loneliness of an untold story of emotional pain. But they don't necessarily have to have been traumatized or hurt in their early years to respond to someone who *listens well*, which is why this is a good strategy for parents, teachers, and other helpers.

To be heard truly and authentically is to be known, and true knowing is different from simple familiarity. It can be easy to be familiar with someone; however, to truly know someone requires the courage to speak with vulnerability and hear with vulnerability. The feelings of the speaker may touch something in us as listener. Mister Rogers had the courage to stay present with his neighbors and did not shy away from listening to difficult conversations. He listened with vulnerability.

The Power of Listening Skills

There are many obstacles that get in the way of true listening. One of these unlikely villains is our own desire;[8] the desire to be heard is often greater than the desire to listen.[9] Our own lack of awareness dupes us into *thinking* we are better listeners than we are.[10] People who seek to bring out the best in others are often taught to cultivate listening skills and self-awareness.[11]

Therapists can certainly be considered professional listeners. It is not fancy therapeutic techniques that account for the most progress in the world of therapy.[12] When people achieve their goals in therapy and are asked how they achieved such success, they often point to characteristics of their therapists. They use words like warm, understanding, and interested to describe them. We use similar words to describe a friend who made us feel heard and understood.[13]

So listening is essential not only for counselors and other "professional listeners" but also for everyone. Early studies on listening suggest that, on average, we tend to spend about 45 percent of our time awake listening in daily life.[14] More specifically, different seasons of life call for even more time listening. For instance, during elementary school. Research suggests students spend nearly 54 percent of their time listening to their teachers, and this only increases during high school and college. Changes in technology including social media, texting, and email are clamoring for our attention and distracting us from being present. The internal noise buzzing in our minds can render us deaf to others, nodding our heads as if to hear while our minds are out to lunch. The noise, both external and internal, challenges our capacity for being emotionally and intellectually present and creates chasms between friends. This epidemic goes far beyond the interpersonal though: the noise and dullness prevents us from tuning in to our own inner voice—missing the beauty, the pain, and the purpose in our own narratives. The noise makes it hard for us to quiet ourselves and tune in to the still, small voice inside, making it nearly impossible to be truly present with our own thoughts, feelings, and stories.

Mister Rogers, America's Television Therapist

Mister Rogers, whom I like to call America's television therapist, cultivated these healing listening skills and desired to know and understand his young neighbors. A story of a young mother and her three-year-old son who were watching *Mister Rogers' Neighborhood* together is just one of many illustrations of this. After Mister Rogers finished his traditional closing by singing "It's Such a Good Feeling," changed out of his cardigan sweater, and reminded viewers how special each of them was, the program ended, and the three-year-old confided in his mother, "Mom, I think he knows my name."[15]

Mister Rogers wasn't a therapist officially, but he consistently had a healing effect on his viewers, comforting them with his personal approach and creating a safe haven so children could explore new parts of themselves and become the best of who they were.[16]

One of the practices that helped him become a healing person was his intentional study to seek to truly *know* his audience.[17] Throughout his years at PBS, Rogers engaged on a weekly basis with his mentor, Dr. Margaret McFarland, to discuss and internalize children's developmental needs. In training counseling students, faculty that teach counseling skills often use a mantra to help students gain more comfort sitting with people in that space between inquiry and answer: "Seek first to understand."

> *Mister Rogers cultivated healing listening skills and desired to know and understand his young neighbors.*

Mister Rogers understood the importance of this principle. He also honed his listening skills in every interaction with the visitors to his PBS neighborhood—children and adults.

Despite being the host of a television program—a position that certainly lends itself to monologue—he still found a way to encourage dialogue. He saw the potential of television and extended a hand, welcoming the challenge to make goodness attractive, including good communication skills. His crew members even jested with him good-naturedly about his rules for talking, which they dubbed "Freddish." He was very careful about how he spoke to children and sought to speak and respond in developmentally appropriate ways.

Mister Rogers's staff members noticed the idiosyncrasies of his scripts and wrote up some instructions on "How to Speak 'Freddish.'"[18] Maxwell King, who wrote a biography on Mister Rogers's life, has written about his discussion with some writers of the *Neighborhood* who assisted with the show. He reported that Mister Rogers was very careful to consider children's ears since they hear words and understand them very literally. In King's discussion with a producer, he learned that Rogers even wanted to rerecord a scene because a nurse had talked about "blowing up" a blood pressure cuff. Rogers, understanding what it is like to have a wild imagination, could sense that children might think that the cuff was going to explode, so he insisted on redoing the scene to change the language to something like "puff it up with air."[19] King summarized the pamphlet that Mister Rogers's cowriters Barry Head and Arthur Greenwald put together in good-natured humor. Speaking Fred's language was a step-by-step process, and they came up with nine specific steps. Here is the essence of them:

1. **State your message** clearly, directly, and in words that are understandable to a preschooler: *It is important to do your schoolwork.*
2. **Rephrase the message in positive terms**: *It is good to do your schoolwork.*
3. **Rework the sentence again**, being mindful that preschool children do not yet have the capacity to make

subtle distinctions: *It is good to do your schoolwork, which includes your homework and other studying that is related to your homework.*

4. **Eliminate any word that is directive or instructive:** *Your teachers will tell you which homework and other work is good to complete today.*

5. **Eliminate sentences that promise certainty;** we cannot really do that: *Your teachers can tell you which homework and related work is good to complete today.*

6. **Rephrase the sentence so that it applies to all children.** Some children may be homeschooled or may not have teachers: *Your favorite grown-ups can suggest which homework and related work may be best to study now.*

7. **Add an idea that provides some motivation or reward** with the instruction: *Your favorite grown-ups can suggest which homework and related work may be best to study now. It is good to get schoolwork suggestions from your favorite adults.*

8. **Rephrase the first statement to eliminate value judgment:** *Your favorite grown-ups can suggest which homework or related work may be best to study. It is important to listen to suggestions from your favorite grown-ups.*

9. **Tie it in to a stage of growth or growing a preschooler can comprehend:** *Your favorite grown-ups can suggest to you what homework to complete and what schoolwork to study. Studying and listening to your favorite grown-ups is an important part of growing.*[20]

Consider how different the commonly stated "You better make sure you do your homework" sounds compared to that last sentence in number nine. Speaking this way certainly requires intentionality and extra effort, but it conveys a caring and empathetic tone.

Listening Well

Mister Rogers approached listening, like he did most things, actively. He described it this way: "Listening is a very active awareness of the coming together of two lives."[21] His listening skills were so sharp, and his ability to relate so strong, that the feeling of connection extended to his television viewers, despite the distance barrier.[22] For the children watching him at home, it was as if Mister Rogers were talking directly to them. This was no accident. He focused on one child at a time and wanted to make a difference for the one. Looking directly into the camera, he asked questions, imagining one child on the other end of the television receiving his questions. Although he could not be present in all our living rooms to hear our answers, he did spend time studying the nature of children so much that children felt personally known by him.

When he met Jeffrey Erlanger, for example, Mister Rogers did the same things he did with all his television viewers:

- He made sure he could make direct eye contact (the first and most important listening skill).
- He walked right up to Jeffrey and sat down on a step to be at eye level with him in his wheelchair, leaning

forward with an open posture (nonverbal listening skills).

- He greeted Jeffrey with enthusiasm (prizing).
- As Jeffrey demonstrated how he used his wheelchair, Mister Rogers remarked that Jeffrey was controlling it (immediacy).
- He asked what made Jeffrey need the wheelchair (open-ended question) and, like a good counselor, he avoided the word *why*!
- He maintained eye contact to encourage Jeffrey to continue speaking, and, during difficult disclosures, he nodded his head (minimal encouragers).
- He reflected back with a paraphrase of what he was hearing (tracking).
- He asked Jeffrey a probing question about what he did when he was feeling blue (promoting insight).
- When he sang "It's You I Like" with Jeffrey, he improvised the lyrics to say that he liked Jeffrey for who he was deep down, not for his "fancy chair" (prizing, unconditional positive regard).[23]

That's a therapeutically packed ten-minute encounter!

Using the Listening Secret in Your Own Neighborhood

Rogers reflected his interest in his neighbors in other ways as well. Those who wish to understand and help others feel understood can practice these same therapeutic listening skills, to not only hear but also understand the nature of their neighbors. Outwardly, some observable manifestations of Rogers's listening skills arc demonstrated by his open posture, including

- lighting up when greeting him or her (prizing the speaker)
- leaning in toward the speaker
- making eye contact
- indicating interest in knowing more

Good listeners are active, not passive sponges who quietly listen and nod along. Good listeners are more like trampolines, allowing us to bounce ideas off them and gain more height and energy as we go.[24]

Mister Rogers was very thoughtful about his presentation. He looked directly into the camera, and directly into our eyes. Remember, eye contact is the first nonverbal listening skill that is taught to counselors in training and it is also considered the most important of all the listening skills.

Mister Rogers's capacity to use these listening skills to make his viewers feel heard and known initially caught his viewers by surprise. His program was not like other television programs that sometimes revealed a world that feels like a closet crammed full of talkers. In his world, Mister Rogers was a breath of fresh air, providing pauses on his show, using silence, and asking thoughtful questions—even pausing as if to listen to responses. His intentional listening skills lingered in the air of his television program.

> *Good listeners are active, not passive sponges who quietly listen and nod along.*

You can use these methods too. It might help to simply slow down.

Draw out your neighbor's story with your genuine interest in who they are. Don't be afraid of pregnant pauses, so-called because someone is about to give birth to a thought. Mister Rogers took the time to listen, slowed conversations, and gave neighbors the gift of silence they needed to give birth to a thought, lest they miss it or abandon it altogether. He wasn't afraid to broach topics that were awkward, uncomfortable— even painful. Consider some of the questions, which were often invitations, he asked:

- "Won't you be my neighbor?" (an invitation to relationship)
- "Have you ever wondered about apples?" (an invitation to wonder)
- "What do you do when you feel blue?" (an invitation to emotional intelligence and insight)
- "Have you ever seen people get angry and break things?" (an invitation to encourage them to talk about challenging things)

Even his questions conveyed sentiments such as a sense of wonder, a desire to understand, and a courage to be vulnerable in the hearing.

Again, how do we actively participate in listening for what is important? How do we go beyond the surface? Rather than listen to reply, we need to listen to understand.[25] This involves active listening skills, sharing with empathetic presence, and reflecting the content of the speaker's story, their core feelings, and most importantly, their meaning. The interiority of life matters—people's stories and their feelings, and sharing them in order to understand and discover the truth of every one of us. Understanding that every neighbor is worthy of being valued and respected is the first step to listening to truly know and understand our neighbors. This requires not only using standard listening skills, such as open posture, but also requires the posture of our hearts to be open so we can use our nonverbal actions to express a caring and compassionate posture toward our neighbor's story.

KEY TAKEAWAYS

- For some people, *being heard* is the miracle they need. Telling their story can have a healing effect.
- Practice listening to understand.
- Be prepared to ask the uncomfortable question or listen to the uncomfortable story.
- Take the time to truly know—the neighbor, the problem, the facts, the issues—before responding.
- Stifle your need to add your two cents; now is not the time.
- Repeat back or paraphrase to make sure you've understood.
- Ask yourself: Will what I say help me understand my neighbor or help me to *be* understood?
- Validate your neighbor's feelings.
- Consider the miracle question; it may help you find a path to a solution.
- Lean in.
- Make eye contact.
- Slow down.

A CONCEPT TO CONTEMPLATE

Listen with more than your ears; use your heart too. We all need to be truly heard and understood. Have you ever noticed yourself being completely fascinated while hearing your neighbor speak? Did you want to understand them better? What thoughts crossed your mind during those experiences?

Validate Feelings

Feelings Are Mentionable and Manageable

People have said, "Don't cry" to other people for years and years, and all it has ever meant is "I'm too uncomfortable when you show your feelings: Don't cry." I'd rather have them say, "Go ahead and cry. I'm here to be with you."

Fred Rogers, *The World According to Mister Rogers*

*W*hether or not they were directly affected by the events of September 11, 2001, Mister Rogers knew that many children watched everything unfold on TV. In response, he aired a public service announcement. Seated at his piano and looking directly at the camera with an expression of deep concern, he said,

If you grew up with our neighborhood, you may remember how we sometimes talked about difficult things. There were days, even beautiful days that weren't happy. . . . I would like to tell you what I often told you when you were much younger: I like you just the way you are. And what's more, I'm so grateful to you for helping the children in your life to know that you'll do everything you can to keep them safe and to help them express their feelings in ways that will bring healing, in many different neighborhoods.[1]

It would be the last time he spoke to his television neighbors. This was not the only time Mister Rogers made a concerted effort to help children process their feelings about current events. When Robert Kennedy was assassinated, Rogers offered a similar PSA. He entered his television house, not singing, and sat down on the bench where he typically changed his shoes. Looking directly into the camera, he explained violence and how parents and kids might feel about it: "The people who are doing these terrible things are making a lot of other people sad and angry—but when we get sad and angry, you and I, we know what to do with our feelings so we don't have to hurt other people."[2]

Rogers often taught viewers how to *talk about* and *manage* feelings on his show. In psychological literature this is often referred to as *emotional intelligence.* Dr. McFarland taught Rogers that "whatever is mentionable is manageable," which is, at its essence, emotional intelligence—an important skill for people of all ages.[3]

Emotional Intelligence Includes Managing Emotions

Regardless of their age, people need a safe place and a safe way to process their feelings—particularly unpleasant feelings like anger, fear, sadness, and so on. Without skills and support to manage overwhelming painful emotions, some perceive suicide as their only escape. Tragically, suicide is the second leading cause of death for people aged ten to thirty-four, and it is the tenth leading cause of death overall in the United States. There were double the number of suicides as homicides in 2017.[4] If children grow up learning how to regulate their feelings, they emerge as adults who are able to regulate their feelings. If they grow up resorting to violence or substances to regulate feelings, then it is more difficult to adopt new coping skills during adulthood.

This process of learning to manage one's emotions is called developing emotional intelligence. Learning how to *mention* emotions—talk them out in a healthy way—is key. Some children go through trauma, or what some researchers call psychological insults[5]—low-grade trauma that may be inflicted through bullying, harsh words, criticism, interpersonal rejection, emotional abandonment, neglect, or any number of painful experiences—and they have to learn what to do with all those feelings.

Mister Rogers was not afraid to talk about painful and difficult topics and the feelings that went along with them. During one conversation in the Land of Make Believe, the topic of feelings, particularly scary feelings, came up. In this conversation, Mister Rogers and his puppets explored the reason it is important to talk about scary things. They concluded that it makes the feelings a little less scary when you talk about them. That is, when you make them manageable.

Anyone who wants to help others can develop good listening (secret 1) and other skills to encourage those who experience overwhelming feelings to develop emotional intelligence.

Emotion regulation is a lifelong struggle for all of us, and for those with mood disorders the struggle can be lethal. Research reveals that developing and cultivating emotional intelligence is associated with a host of benefits, including

- less emotional effort to comply with job-related emotional demands;[6]
- lower levels of occupational stress;[7]
- positive health outcomes;[8]
- improved relationships;[9]
- improved academic performance;
- improved work performance; and
- lower levels of job-related burnout.[10]

Mister Rogers took the important lesson his mentor taught him and applied it in his television programming. He fearlessly plunged headlong into topics rarely spoken of, such as loneliness, sadness, divorce, anger, and much more. Central to his work was unveiling simple creative practices we can use to express emotions. He taught safe techniques for managing those sometimes painful emotions and experiences. The ability to manage and regulate emotions is a critical part of emotional intelligence, and Mister Rogers was a constant example of these practices.

The Mister Rogers Effect: Making Feelings Mentionable and Manageable

I reference a famous video in part 1 where Fred Rogers appeared before the US Senate Subcommittee on Communications in 1969.[11] The chairman, John Pastore, a self-proclaimed "pretty tough guy," stood between Rogers and the continued level of funding for the Corporation of Public Broadcasting. The Nixon administration sought to route funds toward the Vietnam War and away from public television, cutting the twenty-million-dollar budget in half. A thick tension filled the air in the courtroom where the decision would be made. Pastore's irritation was written all over his face as he began, "All right, Rogers, you've got the floor!"

Rogers began speaking in his customary gentle voice, seemingly unaffected by the senator's irritation. "Senator Pastore, this is a philosophical statement and would take about ten minutes to read, so I'll not do that." He smiled. "One of the first things that a child learns in a healthy family is *trust*, and I trust what you said, that you *will* read this; it is very important to me, I care deeply about children. My first children—"

In a loud, irritated tone, Pastore interrupted. "Will it make you happy if you read it?" Nervous laughter filled the air.

Rogers, maintaining his composure, with even more gentleness and compassion in his voice, replied, "I'd just like to talk about it—if that's okay?"

The soft answer seemed to disarm Senator Pastore. "All right, sir. That's okay." He nodded his head for Rogers to go on.

He continued. "My first program was on WQED fifteen years ago, and its budget was thirty dollars. Now, with the help of the Sears Roebuck Foundation and National Educational Television as well as all of the affiliated stations, each station pays to show our program. It is a unique kind of funding in educational television. With this help, now our program has a budget of six thousand dollars. It may sound like quite a difference, but . . ." Rogers went on to explain that cartoons cost six thousand dollars for less than two minutes of action, with the implication that *Mister Rogers' Neighborhood* was a bargain. But more importantly, the program was good for kids.

It would have been easy for Fred Rogers to feel many unpleasant emotions—threatened, nervous, offended, angry—but he was emotionally intelligent. He didn't argue with Senator Pastore. He did not let emotion overwhelm him. He did not take the senator's tone or mood personally (or as I say when training counseling students, "Remember your QTIP," which stands for "Quit taking it personally").

As Rogers spoke, many eyes in the room began to shift to Pastore, who was listening intently. Rogers went on, "I've worked in the field of child development for six years now, trying to understand the inner needs of children. We deal with such things as the inner drama of childhood. . . . We deal with such things as getting a haircut, or the feelings about brothers and sisters, and the kind of anger that arises in simple family situations, and we speak to it constructively."

Pastore tilted his head, and, matching Rogers's soft tone, wondered, "How long a program is it?"

"A half hour," Rogers responded.

Pastore's demeanor changed as Rogers continued to explain the nature of his program. Rogers explained that a hundred programs had been made "and then when the money ran out people in Boston, and Pittsburgh, and Chicago all came to the floor and said, 'We've *got* to have more of this neighborhood expression of care!' And this is what I give. I give an expression of care every day to each child to help him realize that he is unique. I end the program by saying"—here Rogers looked directly at the senator—"'You've made this day a special day by just your being you. There is no person in the whole world like you, and I like you just the way you are.' And I feel that if we in public television can only make it clear that feelings are mentionable and manageable, we will have done a great service for mental health."

Rogers made comparisons between his program and others that children were offered during the daytime programming hours. He emphasized, "I think that it is much more dramatic that two men could be working out their feelings of anger, much more dramatic than showing something of gunfire. I am constantly concerned about what our children are seeing,

> *If we make it clear that feelings are mentionable and manageable, we will have done a great service for mental health.*

and for fifteen years I have tried, in this country and Canada, to present what I feel is a meaningful expression of care."

After hearing Rogers express his firm belief in the importance of helping children manage feelings, Pastore cut in. "Do you narrate it?"

Rogers said, "I'm the host, yes. And I do all the puppets, and I write all the music, and I write all the scripts."

Pastore, now smiling, said, "Well, I am supposed to be a pretty tough guy, but this is the first time I've had goosebumps in two days!" Laughter broke out on the senate floor. There was transformation in Pastore's eyes; he'd been won over. The Mister Rogers effect was taking shape.

Rogers asked the senator if he could recite the words to one of the songs used in the program. With Pastore's enthusiastic yes, Rogers said, "This has to do with that good feeling of control, which I feel that children need to know is there. And it starts out, 'What do you do with the mad that you feel?' . . . That first line came straight from a child." Rogers went on to recite the rest of the song, including lyrics that conveyed the message that before you do something that could be harmful to another person, you can stop yourself, and instead remember this song.

Pastore was clearly affected. Waving one hand in the air, he said, "I think it's wonderful." Then he said, "Looks like you just earned the twenty million dollars." The room broke out in applause.

This is the Mister Rogers effect—in action once again. The key principle of gratitude (secret 4) combined with other principles like remembering that feelings are mentionable and manageable are tools Rogers used to save public television.

Again, notice that although Rogers may have been addressed in an abrupt, gruff way and was made to feel hurried, he never lost his composure. He did not outwardly exhibit frustration. Instead Rogers managed his irritation and was able to connect with the irritation Pastore felt and share a relevant song and message. In just a few minutes, the emotionally intelligent Rogers had a transformative effect on the senator and won twenty million dollars for public broadcasting. Rogers's ability to respond with intentionality, and in a spirit of peace, speaks to his inner strength.

> *Rogers's ability to respond with intentionality, and in a spirit of peace, speaks to his inner strength.*

The Psychology of Emotion Management

For those who have problems regulating their mood, who struggle with discouragement or have mood disorders such as depression, interpersonal challenges (for example, giving a speech or confronting hostility or being questioned), regulating emotions may seem overwhelming. People who struggle with persistent sadness in the form of clinical depression are more likely to withdraw from conflicts within their relationships and to avoid interpersonal challenges altogether, even with loved ones. Mister Rogers's interaction with Pastore illustrates the capacity he had to regulate his mood and emotions and manage feelings of sadness even when facing impending loss (such as the potential changes in public television). Instead of reacting to Senator Pastore's demeanor, he redirected his emotions into productive engagement with the senator. These skills served him well in his capacity to effect change, bring out the best in Pastore, and make a difference.

Researchers who have investigated the interpersonal basis of mood disorders, such as chronic depression, have found that those who struggle with these conditions tend to have difficulties identifying the relational consequences of their actions, which can lead to a lack of awareness of how they impact their environment. Negative results leave them feeling paralyzed and unlikely to take action to effect interpersonal change. Some psychologists call this phenomenon interpersonal sameness, and it often arises from a history filled with painful relational experiences called psychological insults.[12]

So developing good and strong emotional intelligence is to be desired. It is important for people to be aware of how their expressions of emotion may influence others in their environment. Emotion management skills can be learned at any age, but as with most things in life, it can be challenging to adopt new skills when it requires unlearning other behaviors or coping mechanisms. Thus secret 2 affects many aspects of human endeavors.

For example, a team of researchers at a university in central Virginia conducted research exploring the connection between emotional intelligence and burnout and found that they are negatively correlated. In other words, as people increased in emotional intelligence, their likelihood of burnout in their work decreased.[13] So it is not only beneficial to others when we help them know their feelings are mentionable and manageable but it is also protective for us. Although researchers looked at all fifteen traits that emotional intelligence comprises—empathy, emotional perception, emotion expression, relationships, emotion management (helping manage emotions of others), assertiveness, self-awareness, self-esteem, optimism, happiness, emotion regulation (managing one's own emotions), low impulsiveness, stress management, adaptability, self-motivation[14]—a few traits were more closely linked with decreases in burnout than others. The self-control factor—an umbrella that covers the capacity to control our own emotions, manage our stress, and maintain low levels of impulsivity—

The self-control factor revealed the most potential to protect us from burnout.

was the factor that revealed the most potential to protect us from burnout.[15] In other words, as the flight attendants say, put on your oxygen mask first before helping others with their masks. This is easy for us helpers to forget, but it applies to parents, teachers, grandparents, coaches, and other helpers who can easily fall prey to professional burnout.

How Was Mister Rogers So Successful at Emotion Regulation?

If we are preoccupied with our own feelings, it is difficult to tend to those of another person. But Mister Rogers had a whole neighborhood to tend. He was awake to their needs and their feelings, and to his own. How did he do it? There was a man with real needs behind the cardigan sweaters. Fred Rogers had at least seven different "built-in" practices that helped him to mention and manage his own emotions:

1. Have someone to talk to
2. Spend time in nature
3. Seek regular solitude
4. Read regularly for inspiration
5. Express yourself artistically
6. Encourage yourself
7. Rest

Rogers was able, as we've discussed, to put his own oxygen mask on first before moving on to help others with theirs.

Have Someone to Talk To

As is the case in counselor training, Rogers engaged in role reversal and met with a psychiatrist to talk about his thoughts and feelings in a safe place. I encourage my students who are studying to be therapists to take time to sit in the other chair, where they'll learn to cultivate empathy and have a safe place to communicate feelings. Sitting in the client's seat also gives counselors an opportunity to voice their concerns and struggles and set them aside during sessions to focus on those of their clients. I, along with many of my peers, can attest to this.

You may choose to confide in a trusted friend or relative. It is important to select a safe person, meaning they are a keeper of secrets and willing to process your thoughts and feelings without offering unsolicited advice (or at least are not offended if you make your own choices and forsake their unsolicited advice). Therapists are recommended, of course, but safe friends can also have a way of being therapeutic.

Spend Time in Nature

Rogers spent time in nature, specifically at the edge of the ocean. Fred and Joanne Rogers had a home at the end of a sand road on Nantucket Island—it was a wedding gift. The house was right on the beach, where Rogers could walk, swim, read, write, and even have chats with friends. Researchers have found that spending time near the ocean is associated with lower levels of stress and increased well-being.[16] However, other "blue spaces"—like a lake pond or pool—can have a therapeutic effect too. Nature can be therapeutic, so if you cannot bathe in the sea, consider a nature walk or some time sitting outside soaking up vitamin D and experiencing the nurturing impact of our natural world.

Seek Regular Solitude

Rogers understood the importance of having his own quiet place where he could be alone to write and reflect. Nantucket was one of his destinations to carve out white space to think and process his experiences.[17] Even if it is too hard to get away, we can try to find pockets of solitude in our day to be present, to write in a journal, or reflect on an inspirational reading.

Read Regularly for Inspiration

Rogers was a man of faith, and each day he would spend time reading his Bible and praying. He was able to process both his burdens and his joys—and those of his neighbors too—through prayer. It was not just his entry into his neighborhood home that was characterized by ritual. His everyday routine was consistent. He got up at 5:30 a.m. and spent time praying and reading the Bible before he was off to his morning swim before work. He ended each day with a 9:30 p.m. bedtime as well.[18] We, too, can implement our own routines into our daily lives. Perhaps a place to start is with adding a consistent time to read inspirational texts and engage in spiritual practices that are meaningful to us.

Express Yourself Artistically

Rogers used music and other artistic forms of expression to process his feelings. When young Fred was sick and had to spend time alone during the summers, he found ways to express himself with puppets and by playing piano. He retained some of these practices in adulthood. He often shared how he could cry through his fingertips on the piano or pound out his anger by playing more aggressively. As he took time to express his feelings and give himself space, he was able to help his neighbors do the same. We can also find outlets for artistic expression. Mister Rogers encouraged children to draw, exercise, play music, use puppets, and engage in whatever creative outlet that suited them. Likewise, I often encourage my clients to try something new, like expressing themselves through Play-Doh or art, which can often allow them to connect with the child within.

Encourage Yourself

Mister Rogers took time to encourage himself. He kept words of affirmation he received from loved ones in his planner or up on his wall to gently remind himself that he could be loved for who he was. He was not surrounded with uplifting words by accident—this was his habit. What is your favorite quote? Consider putting it on a Post-it note on your computer monitor, on a note in your phone, or in your planner. Some Adlerian psychologists would say that your favorite quote is your advice to yourself, and some career counselors would say it is the title of your career story.[19] It can be therapeutic to tap into your own wisdom in moments when unpleasant or painful emotions take hold. This can help with self-soothing and emotional regulation.

Rest

The same Mister Rogers who produced more than eight hundred television programs and wrote barrels of songs and several books also rested. He told his journalist friend Tom Junod that he slept eight hours a night from 9:30 p.m. to 5:30 a.m., and that he took a nap in the afternoons. He practiced activities that helped put his mind, his heart, and his soul to rest—this likely made it easier to get a nourishing night's sleep.

Of course, this is not all Mister Rogers did—he had many other adaptive habits, like his humor, swimming each morning, and working at a comfortable pace (he liked to take his time). He was able to face the truths of his pleasant and painful feelings, and people who knew him have remarked that he was true to himself. On-screen, Mister Rogers played himself: the truth of his vulnerable emotions shared through Daniel Tiger, his powerful emotions shown through King Friday, and beginning and ending each show with messages of love and acceptance—no puppets needed—for all his neighbors. He taught us that all our feelings are mentionable and manageable, and he modeled ways to share them and connect emotionally with our neighbors.

Using the Validating Feelings Secret in Your Own Neighborhood

There are obstacles that can make it difficult to operate in an emotionally intelligent way. These hurdles—which can manifest as emotions, personality types, or both—emerge on the journey to an emotionally intelligent and emotionally regulated approach to life. Parents, teachers, and other helpers might consider these potential snags and determine how best to handle them.

Using Unpleasant Phrasing

One of the first obstacles to emotional intelligence is the many messages that are commonplace in American culture that communicate *feelings are not mentionable*. Although the oft-heard admonition to "turn that frown upside down" may seem innocent, it is anything but. Other such phrases include

- "Put a smile on your face."
- "Don't frown or your face will get stuck that way."
- "Don't complain or I'll give you something to complain about."

These phrases seem to teach emotional regulation, or surface acting (demonstrating feelings that are consistent with what one thinks is expected of them), which can create long-term emotional challenges. Indeed, they teach that feelings are not mentionable or manageable, nor is it safe to talk about them with others.

Instead, we can seek to **validate** feelings, especially with children, so they grow into adults with a healthy approach to emotions. For example, we can say, "It looks like you're feeling frustrated." This includes identifying the feeling word and voicing it in order to acknowledge it.

We can also **empathize**: "It can be really frustrating when you are all set to go in one direction, and your teacher changes the instructions." Don't rush to fix it. Take a moment to just "be with" the person in his or her feelings.

An alternative option is to **sit with it**: You may say, "Some people feel frustration like a wave of heat while others say they can feel their heart beat faster. Help me understand what it feels like for you."

Choose to **work on it**: "Are you comfortable sharing more about what is frustrating you?" Or, "How would you like to express your frustration?" For example, Mister Rogers would pound out his mad feelings on the piano or vigorously swim laps in the pool.

Or with young children, perhaps we can borrow a line from Mister Rogers's television offspring Daniel Tiger: "When you feel so mad that you could roar, take a deep breath and count to four."[20]

Rejection and Dismissal of Emotions

People who develop a dismissing attachment style (see "A World without Mister Rogers") tend to, as the name suggests, turn away from relationships, mentioning feelings, or just about anything that feels like connection or intimacy. They often have histories characterized by rejection. People pushed them away. Their expressions of pain and hurt may have been dismissed, minimized, or laughed at. Repeated experiences of rejection over time can cause a person to turn away from relationship figures and focus on independence and strength rather than vulnerability and connection. In its most severe form, this relationship style can lead to complete isolation. Expressing any need is seen as weakness, and strength and independence are highly valued.

If you encounter someone like this, remember QTIP (quit taking it personally). Instead, try to evoke compassion and patience, and visualize the person as a child crying and being turned away again and again and again. Provide many assurances of safety, which might sound something like this: "You do not have to share anything that makes you feel uneasy, but I want to give you a safe place to discuss your feelings if you are comfortable doing so."

Likewise, if you recognize dismissing aspects in your own relational style, remember that change takes time. Give yourself credit for reading thus far and even pondering the thought of interpersonal situations and emotions. Remember that avoiding emotions means shutting out not only the unpleasant emotions but also positive emotions, such as joy and intimacy. It also means shutting out true intimacy and connection. Engaging feelings, especially when it's a new experience, can be uncomfortable, but consistently doing so allows progress to be made. It may be difficult to trust others with your emotions, and it may be difficult to be present with the emotions of others at first.

Getting Tangled Up in Feelings

While some of us grow up avoiding emotions and emotional availability, people on the other end of the spectrum grow up flooded and overwhelmed by emotion. How does this happen, that a child becomes quickly overwhelmed or overly dramatic when expressing emotions? Well, one way this pattern develops is when a child's first relational figures engaged in role reversal, making a bid for the child to care for the parent's emotions. For example, "Mommy feels sad when you cry, and when you bring Mommy flowers, Mommy feels happy." Another pathway to this entanglement is inconsistency, such that sometimes the parent is very loving and other times they are unloving, rejecting, or neglectful. The child does not know exactly what to expect and is confused. The child has to become dramatic in order to earn the parent's attention and care. This can lead to the development in early life of expressing emotions in a more dramatic or exaggerative way, or alternatively in a fearful or passive manner.

If you find you have a tendency to be easily overwhelmed by feelings or circumstances, there is hope. It is important to self-monitor and notice when you are feeling lost in emotion. As you develop this awareness, you can identify triggers. For example, when you are tired after a long day it may be more difficult to have conversations with your spouse about his or her requests. If you are in the midst of a conflict with another person, we know that it can take about twenty minutes to calm down and have a productive conversation. Some experts suggest excusing yourself to the restroom with a book to give your heart rate a chance to come down.

But that is not the only reason you may want to head for the restroom. Dr. Marsha Linehan has identified and compiled some research-based skills for activating the parasympathetic nervous system—the system within our bodies that helps calm us and decrease physiological arousal.[21] The classic example is to splash cold water on your face; it's more effective if you hold your breath.

Linehan suggests a series of other skills that can work to change our physiological state, including physical exercise, breathing exercises, and progressive muscle relaxation. She developed a mnemonic device to make them easier for her clients to remember. They are called TIP skills, which stands for Temperature Intense Exercise.[22] It turns out Rogers's suggestion in his song about "rounding up friends for a game of tag" and seeing how fast you can run is apropos, because getting your heart rate up can help change your physiological state.

Avoiding Mixed Messages about Sadness

Some may have heard messages that sadness is a sign of weakness, or that "boys don't cry." But feelings communicate important messages, as Mister Rogers taught and emotional intelligence research supports. Sadness and tears at the loss of a loved one do not communicate weakness but rather the valuing of one who is lost. This valuing is associated with secure attachment behavior. Loss is inherently disorganizing, and when someone loses a loved one, this external change requires an internal shift to adjust to the change. For example, those who grew up watching *Mister Rogers' Neighborhood* and valuing Mister Rogers's influence may feel a sense of sadness and loss that he is no longer with us and may seek to find ways to honor his legacy. This sadness communicates the great value of Rogers's life and influential messages.[23]

There are as many kinds of sadness as there are ways to address it. Start with **validating** and **accepting**: "I see the sadness in your eyes. It is okay to cry."

Listening is always a good idea: "If those tears had words, what would they say?"

Many of us struggle with "the right thing to say" to someone who is sad, but sometimes simply sitting quietly and being with the person is enough. We are often tempted to rush in and try to fix the situation or give unsolicited advice, but being willing to sit with a person in their time of sadness or grief can be a great source of comfort. Often just in the process of being present, things get accomplished. An old proverb says, "Shared joy is doubled and sorrow shared is halved." Sharing has a healing impact.

Make Anger Manageable Too

When I was in college I saw anger managed appropriately. My grandmother was disrespected by a young man, and she let him know in no uncertain terms that she would not stand for it . . . without so much as raising her voice. Not everyone knows how to do this. It was a perfect example of how to express anger appropriately—that is, no one was yelled at, injured, or disrespected.

A little boy who was discussing his feelings of anger with Mister Rogers asked him, "What do you do with the mad that you feel?" As Mister Rogers told Senator Pastore, he wrote a song about the boy's question and his answer, in which he provides suggestions such as pounding on some clay or gathering friends to play a cardiovascular game of tag and then seeing how fast you could run. The song reminds listeners that it is possible to stop a tantrum before it goes too far—that they can use self-control. The animated show *Daniel Tiger's Neighborhood* tells kids in a similar song that "when you feel so mad that you could roar, take a deep breath and count to four." In just one line, children learn a strategy to keep in mind for managing their feelings.

It's important to remember that anger can be triggered by many things—trouble at school or at work, anxiety or stress, even frustration—and solutions for calming the waters are just as varied. The TIP skills discussed previously apply here as well. Some may find twenty minutes of aerobic exercise at an intense level does the trick. Sometimes anger arises because we refuse to accept the reality of a situation, or maybe we decide we must get to the restaurant by six o'clock, then get stuck in a traffic jam that we cannot control. The sooner we adjust and practice radical acceptance, the better. It can be relieving to remember that even if things do not go as we wished, nothing tragic has happened and the world is not over.

KEY TAKEAWAYS

- If we can talk about unpleasant or overwhelming feelings, then they can be managed.
- Feelings can be uncomfortable but learning to manage them is an important skill for people of all ages.
- Emotional intelligence includes managing feelings.
- Emotional intelligence improves relationships, health, and academic performance.
- Emotional intelligence lowers levels of occupational stress and burnout.
- Validation of feelings is an important component of managing emotions, so ask, confirm, validate, emphasize, and talk about your emotions.
- We can engage or disengage from a feeling based on its utility.
- We can learn practices to help us manage our emotions well. Such practices range from solitude and physical exercise to engaging in creative pursuits.

A CONCEPT TO CONTEMPLATE

Feelings are mentionable and manageable. Validation of emotions helps us learn to regulate our moods and develop emotional intelligence.

A good first step is to start labeling our own feelings through journaling and move toward caring for our feelings so we can be present with others. If you were to label your feelings, what emotions are you experiencing as you read?

Pause and Think

Take Time to Discover What Is Inside

Here is my secret. It's quite simple: One sees clearly
only with the heart. Anything essential is invisible to
the eyes.

Antoine de Saint-Exupéry, The Little Prince

*B*y 1991 the *Neighborhood* had been on the air for
over twenty years, and Fred and Joanne Rogers
were still carefully answering every fan letter, every "Yes!"
to Mister Rogers's invitation to be neighbors. Not a single
piece of mail from a television neighbor went unanswered.
Rogers took the time to answer each letter he received with
great thoughtfulness and intentionality.

One night, Rogers opened a letter from someone who
was interested in knowing what books had influenced him

over the years. That was easy: the first book on Rogers's top-ten list was Antoine de Saint-Exupéry's *The Little Prince*.[1] Beloved by millions worldwide—it has been translated into three hundred languages and dialects[2]—*The Little Prince* is a parable that addresses universal themes of human nature: fear, uncertainty, loneliness, love, and friendship. It contained words Rogers lived by and reminded himself and his guests of regularly.

There is one passage from *The Little Prince* that particularly moved Mister Rogers. (You can see it at the beginning of this chapter.) He kept a framed version of this quote, written in calligraphy and displayed in the original French, beside his office chair at WQED in Pittsburgh[3]—along with children's artwork sent by television neighbors and some other inspirational quotes.[4]

But why did Fred Rogers identify so strongly with this insight? How did he know that what is essential about each of us as a person is what we hold inside us, what you can't see by simply looking? He had an inside story too.

Fred Rogers grew up shy, struggling with many childhood sicknesses, and he also struggled with his weight. He was teased, taunted, and bullied. He was vulnerable and the only son of protective parents. Before his family adopted his sister when Fred was eleven years old, he spent a lot of time alone.

And yet . . . he took this pain and turned it into purpose, and all his television neighbors were enriched by it. But *how* is it that young Freddy of Westmoreland County, Pennsylvania, became the man all of America knew as Mister Rogers?

It might have been this incident. One day school let out early at Latrobe Elementary, and Freddy didn't have a ride home. He began walking the ten blocks to his house. But then he heard footsteps behind him, picking up speed. He began running as he heard the voices attached to the footsteps— and they were shouting insults. The voices were those of a group of young boys who'd been picking on him for weeks.

Pounding feet and cruel words echoed in his ears as the boys closed in on him, shouting, "Freddy, hey, fat Freddy. We're going to get you, Freddy."[5]

Fred found refuge that day with a family he knew. Out of breath, he pounded on the door and was let in, finding safety with this good neighbor. The neighbor called Freddy's family to have someone come to pick him up. Something inside young Freddy was released that day, and I believe it was the beginning of his transformation into Mister Rogers.

Young Fred felt resentful that those boys didn't see past his physical appearance or his shyness.[6] Meanwhile, trusted adults told him if he pretended not to care, the bullies would likely stop bothering him. It was no solution.

His grandfather Fred McFeely, the man he was named for, often said to him, "Freddy, you made this day a special day for me just by your being you."[7] Over time, Fred got the message: people could like him for who he was on the inside because the fabric of his being was good. He took both his painful and his redeeming experiences and found a healing way to move forward.

> *He took both his painful and his redeeming experiences and found a healing way to move forward.*

What Is Essential?

We could hypothesize that these painful experiences—being bullied and having many childhood sicknesses, including scarlet fever, which kept Fred inside sick for weeks at a time[8]—made for a childhood that had its challenges. But each trial was a character-building experience, and the time he spent alone helped him consider what was truly important to a fulfilling life.

Perhaps these experiences led Fred to develop important values to live by, which emerged continuously throughout his work. Perhaps he began to understand what was, in fact, essential:

- Look past outward appearances to search for the rest of the story (the essential) in each person—even yourself. Rogers gleaned his concept from his favorite text and beloved quote.
- When tempted to judge someone's outward appearance, take time to wonder what that person has gone through. He kept another quote in his wallet to remind himself that he could learn to love anyone if he just heard their story.[9]
- Demeaning behavior is hurtful and destructive. There is nothing that sparked more anger in Fred Rogers than people treating others poorly. He channeled his anger productively by offering an alternative avenue of television that differed from the injustice seen on the programs that were offered to children.
- Make goodness attractive. He believed searching for the good was a holy quest.

- Have compassion for each person's inside story, even if it is a painful one. Sit with them in their pain.
- It is okay to feel the whole range of emotions. Sharing feelings in appropriate ways is an important theme that that Rogers used throughout his programming.
- We all have choices about how we respond to the painful parts of our stories.
- Cultivate curiosity—about people and the world. He sought to do this through his field trips and his questions.
- Take time to process what you learn about the invisible essential before drawing conclusions.

White Space and the Invisible Essential

One of the themes of Rogers's work was the idea that the unseen is more valuable than the seen. He viewed this in several different senses:

- What is inside us is more valuable than what is outside.
- The white space around the paragraphs is more important than the text "because it allows you to think about what has just been said."[10]
- Being is more important than doing.

Mister Rogers understood that a simple, quiet, contemplative, and reflective way of life was far better than a complicated, frenzied way of life. He brought an inner calm and peace to his program and his life, and he was even concerned that our society as a whole was more interested in noise than silence, in information than wonder. He invited us to unsubscribe from the idea that more is more and consider that sometimes less can be more, and deep and simple is a better way.

The typical definition of white space refers to portions of a typed page that are intentionally left blank—most commonly, the margins. Rogers used this term both literally and figuratively to refer to the blank space on a page, the space used to contemplate profound concepts such as forgiveness, the silent pauses in our dialogues, and the time to pause and reflect on things that are happening.[11]

Mister Rogers valued this white space, as he valued the "essential" quote from *The Little Prince*. It is not surprising what his first influential book turned out to be!

What does it mean to you that what is most essential in life cannot be seen by the eye? It is concepts like these that merit "white space" for contemplation. In fact, to Mister Rogers, the Presbyterian minister, it was biblical. In the Psalms, the Hebrew word *selah* is frequently used. Some scholars believe *selah* to mean "pause and think of that."[12] The book he deemed greatest, the Bible, regularly encourages taking white space.

I can imagine that when Mister Rogers, an avid reader, took time to read his favorite books, he would pause and think of the words he'd just read. This space for reflection, too, is white space. Rogers emphasized the great gift of silence and how those who made a difference for him often gave him silence.[13]

In an interview, the curious and inquisitive Mister Rogers also paused to inquire of his interviewer Charlie Rose, a

practice that was typical of him. He wondered, "How do we
. . . encourage reflection? How do we make goodness attractive?" Even in his way of speaking, Rogers left intentional
short white spaces for contemplation. He revealed to Charlie
that he took quiet time for reflection each morning. At the
beginning of the interview, Charlie asked questions with the
speed of a machine gun. By the end of the interview, Mister
Rogers had clearly affected him; Charlie began admiring
Mister Rogers's state of calm and remarking on it. They
began connecting more deeply and reflecting on making a
difference, and Charlie even slowed his rate of speech, play-
fully protesting, "You're turning this around on me!" Yet
Charlie was compelled to explore Rogers's questions, like
invitations to dive into the deep end of a pool of meaning.
Charlie, too, was transformed in that moment by the Mister
Rogers effect—his attitude and pace changed.[14]

Despite all the things that Rogers had to *do*, such as serv-
ing as the puppeteer, scriptwriter, narrator, and musical
composer of his show and responsibilities such as writing
letters, visiting with viewers, and many other tasks, he still
valued *being*. Rogers regularly took time to slow down and
take some white space for reflection, whether by reflecting
on concepts that he read, going away to his summer home
in Nantucket to reflect and write, or taking a weekend away
to think and pray.

Mister Rogers believed that the more we know and make
this key principle (what is essential is invisible to the eye)
a part of us, the closer we get to true wisdom and neigh-
borliness.[15] Rogers devoted time to self-discovery and con-
templating such truths and what they meant for him and
for others.

The Mister Rogers Effect: The Effects of the Invisible

Mister Rogers had a fascination with the stories inside all of us—even himself. He used reflection (white space) and journaling to follow his own story and work through what is often called writer's block. We have a record of one such time when he wrestled with his creative process and turned to journaling to process his concerns. In a note, Rogers reflected on the challenge, where he disclosed his feelings of doubt. On what appears to be a yellow piece of paper, the inquisitive Mister Rogers handwrote his thoughts, asking himself a question (which was often his way of initiating things): "Am I kidding myself that I am able to write a script again?"

He continued by typing up his thoughts as he wondered about the answer to this question, reflected on the feeling of agony associated with creating, and challenged himself: "I wonder if every creative artist goes through the tortures of the damned trying to create? Oh well, the hour cometh and now IS when I've got to do it. GET TO IT, FRED!"

He closed his note with a caution not to let anyone ever suggest that the process was easy; he emphasized that it was not!

Three weeks later, he took the time to follow up with a handwritten memo explaining what he learned from the experience. It read, "It wasn't easy but it was good. The five new scripts about school are nearly complete and I can see how helpful they can be. This I must remember!"[16]

He encouraged himself and this self-talk illustrates the wisdom of looking within during the creative process. As he wrote in his memo, he took time to remind himself that his work was not easy, but it was good. It is comforting to know that even Mister Rogers, despite all his success and creativity, had episodes of doubt and struggled with the process. Journaling his thoughts gave him an opportunity, not only to take white space for reflection but also to mention his feelings and manage them. He was gracious and courageous enough to let his humanity be seen, lest we think he was perfect. He found solace in encouraging and reminding himself of the truth, inoculating himself against future encounters with doubt.

> *He took time to remind himself that his work was not easy, but it was good.*

A former student of mine, now a sought-after counselor, was tuned in to the advantages of journaling too. Arnold was not a native English speaker, yet he consistently spoke eloquently and with precision. When I asked how he did it, he shared his secret with a smile: "Well, when I was about twelve years old, I started reading, reflecting, and journaling every day. I noticed a direct correlation between my ability to articulate myself and the time I spent doing these things. When I slack off on reading and journaling, I begin to notice that I have more difficulty in expressing my thoughts." There are many advantages to setting aside white space in your schedule; reflection—whether you journal it, thinking the solution through, or just mull it over briefly—offers clarity that can't be achieved any other way.

We can see how Mister Rogers's calm, reflective tendencies helped him to listen and remain centered and open to his neighbors—sometimes, perhaps, being a little too curious for comfort. Rogers was famous for developing friendships with journalists and being delightfully challenging to interview.

One journalist who had interacted with Rogers wrote an essay that was inspired by his favorite quotation from *The Little Prince*. Writer Jeanne Marie Laskas, in her essay "What Is Essential Is Invisible to the Eye," described the effect Rogers had on her: "You think you are learning about him, but all of a sudden you realize you're learning about yourself. That, of course is fascinating so you stay with it. And pretty soon Fred is invisible; it's just you in the room, facing you."[17] Mister Rogers was not satisfied with surface-level connection; he insisted on depth and helped others to find more depth in themselves.

Fred Rogers loved people and their stories. His appreciation of white space and his commitment to discovering invisible essentials (including spiritual essentials)—the truest things about us, like our vulnerable thoughts, our deepest feelings, and our spiritual values—allowed him to create space for others to talk about difficult topics, like divorce, without judgment. Rogers's wife, Joanne, revealed, "He had a heart that had room for everyone, and he was fascinated by other people's journeys."[18] His friend Tim Madigan also described the way he saved room in his spirit for others: "Fred wanted to know the truth of your life, the nature of your insides, and he had room enough in his own spirit to embrace without judgment whatever that truth might be."[19]

Mister Rogers loved all of his neighbors and wanted to reach people of all socioeconomic, racial, and religious backgrounds, and his own faith played an important role in his value system. He believed that the sacred was at work between what was emitted from the television and what viewers heard or felt. It is important to remember that a holistic approach to seeing people includes seeing their spiritual needs as well and making room for the sacred.

The Psychology of Cultivating a Desire for the Essential

The impact of extended understanding and awareness of oneself is tremendous—it is its own reward, as we have seen in how Fred Rogers made sense of his childhood trauma to serve him and others for the better. Clearly, it was important to Rogers to discover the inner truth about himself and others. And it's all well and good to note we *should* seek the unseen essential. But how do we cultivate that desire—in ourselves, our children, and others we hope to help?

It helps if you have learned how to have healthy relationships.

One of the greatest predictors of whether we develop a secure style of relating to others is determined by our capacity to make sense of our attachment history—that is, our interpersonal (relationship) history (see "A World without Mister Rogers"). After extensive training and fifteen years writing about, researching, and teaching on the topic of attachment, if I could simplify what I have learned about how secure attachment develops, the key message would be this: Children need responsive and available caregivers. These caregivers do not need to be perfect but "good enough" in terms of being available, sensitive, and responsive. If this is the case, childhood generally provides enough white space (unstructured time) for children to make sense of their own stories. Unfortunately, only about 62 percent of the "normal" population of infants tend to have responsive and available caregivers that help them develop a secure style of relating.[20]

Without consistent interactions with a responsive caregiver, an insecure attachment style can develop. However, people are not stuck with the attachment style they have; they can make it more secure.[21] In other words, you can change, and you can help others to change.

In order to move toward a secure style of interacting in relationships in adulthood, the most important step one can take is to make sense of the past in a way that is characterized by balance, forgiveness, and an honest and clear capacity to accept your story for what it is and communicate it clearly. In other words, you need to develop understanding about the truth of your story, and as you face the truth, develop a fresh, consistent, and clear narrative so that you can share it with others in a way that makes sense. Remember, according to attachment research, you are not stuck with the relationship style you have. You can develop it and make it better. Facing the truth of your story is one of the most adaptive ways you can move from an insecure attachment style to a secure style of relating.

Discovery, Wonderment, and the Invisible Essential

Mister Rogers was a proponent of using white space to help people cultivate their imagination and creativity. He understood the benefits inherent in these practices. Research has revealed that children who grew up watching Mister Rogers tend to have longer levels of persistence related to school activities than those who watched other programming.[22] Why? One key factor was pacing. Because the program unfolded at a pace that allowed children to process what they were seeing and learning, it cultivated time for wonder and space for reflection.

Rogers courageously challenged the pressure to produce fast-paced television. He did this by pausing on public television during his program to show children how long a minute really is by timing it and silently waiting for it to pass.

Mister Rogers did not just slow down with children. He was also willing to ask a large adult television audience to pause and take ten seconds of silence (while he kept time) in order to give the audience a chance to think of and thank those people who had loved them into becoming themselves. Rogers stood out in this fast-paced world because he created space and time for what was important.[23] He understood the pace that children needed and the importance of taking his time and allowing for some white space.

Mister Rogers's priority of providing time for reflection and silence to grow things (such as ideas) in the "Garden of Your Mind"[24] (as he sang about in one of his neighborhood songs) was a strong theme throughout his work. He often used the counseling skill we call "reflecting meaning" to identify what was meaningful in his neighbor's narrative and allow for space to contemplate it. His willingness to examine his own story and to parent his inner child in a kind, compassionate way gave him the space and knowledge to help provide that same caring voice to others.

Mister Rogers was interested in the deeply internal values, feelings, and thoughts of his neighbors, but he also cultivated wonder and interest in everyday outside things too. He made space for small wonderment by taking time to pause and really see what was around him with fresh eyes and to marvel at all that made it good. Discovery, wonderment, and the search for the invisible happen in this white space, the margin that we have *when we take our time.*

Children are often good at marveling and expressing curiosity as they discover new information until they are squeezed by their environments and inhibition is acquired to prevent them from expressing wonderment or asking questions that may inconvenience others. Caring adults might recall the "There are no dumb questions" admonishment from high school chemistry class and rework it—"Your questions show you are learning"—for impressionable children.

Mister Rogers wondered about everyday things, including how apple juice is made (since you cannot squeeze apples like you can oranges), and how pinball machines are created. Experiences of silence, wonderment, marvel, savoring, and discovery are all too rare in our noisy world.

In the field of positive psychology, this sense of curiosity that drives contemplation and wonderment is not only considered a personal characteristic but is also conceptualized as a "signature strength." Curiosity is part of the "wisdom and knowledge" cluster of strengths and involves an openness to the world around us, especially to things that do not fit into our preconceived notions of how things should be. This wide-eyed approach to environment can be narrow and specific to certain niches or broad and encompassing of the global experience. Some ideas for adding wonderment and curiosity to our lives include taking time to read or listen to audiobooks and wonder about things in the white space or margins, reading books with some discussion questions, and taking nature walks and stopping to look at flowers or gaze at birds in flight with awe and wonder.

As a function of his time spent studying and consulting, Rogers understood the pace that children needed and how important it was to take his time and allow for some white space. He lived in a way that was consistent with his values, and he was determined to do what was best for his young viewers. He was even willing to swim upstream against the pressures of the television world to maintain this priority.

While other television stations were showing fast-paced scenes of fighting and gunfire, Mister Rogers retained the slow, steady space and facilitation of discovery that was characteristic of the child-friendly wonder of the neighborhood.

Using the Pause and Think Secret in Your Own Neighborhood

Some people go through painful experiences and become bitter or angry; others go through similar experiences and turn their pain into purpose somehow. We have choices about how we respond to the painful parts of our own stories, but finding purpose in pain begins with reflection in the white space moments. Sometimes we find that suffering develops a place in our hearts that was not there before. Fred Rogers left a sick, unhappy childhood behind and became Mister Rogers, a television neighbor beloved by millions.

Stories abound of young people who lost a parent or sibling to a terrible disease and later went to medical school to learn how to develop a cure. We might point to Elie Wiesel, who survived the Holocaust in Auschwitz as a teenager and went on to become a professor, author, and activist for human rights. He won the Nobel Prize for Peace in 1986.[25] A sufferer of chronic depression himself, Professor James McCullough helped revolutionize the treatment of depression, helping more than 450 patients diagnosed with chronic depression. His memoir is a "life trajectory of hope."[26]

> *Finding purpose in pain begins with reflection in the white space moments.*

Often those who suffer find a protector or friend who offers kindness. Sometimes it is a wise elder who helps the sufferer make sense of his or her feelings, to let them know it is okay to be sad—even angry—and to talk with them about their feelings.

In essence, Mister Rogers learned to be who he had needed as a child, or as some psychologists would say, he learned how to serve as his own compassionate parent.[27] Helpers can listen, acknowledge, validate, empathize, encourage, and help those who suffer make sense of their pain. This journey can lead to a heightened self-awareness and, in many cases, it can provide the safe space a person needs to develop self-compassion and experience healing.

Discovering the invisible in oneself is what therapists often refer to as *self-awareness*. It requires taking a good honest look at your internal psychological processes, such as thoughts, feelings, motivations, and behaviors. How do you become self-aware? Taking some white space, or quiet time, to reflect and contemplate is the key to increasing self-awareness. You can also achieve that goal by taking time to consider your perceptions and process your experiences.[28]

Another way Fred Rogers took time to engage in contemplative reflection was via writing. He was not alone in experiencing the benefits of putting pen to page—from tracking dreams to journaling stressful events to keeping a book of creative ideas or plans. Writing it all down can make sense of it (whatever *it* is). Writing allows you to mention your feelings and manage them. Some creatives journal first thing upon arising; some contemplatives like to take stock at the end of the day. Regardless, you can increase your self-awareness by writing yourself into a state of enhanced perceptiveness. In training counselors and therapists, I have noticed that students who have exceptionally strong counseling skills tend to take time to journal and reflect.

Those who don't enjoy writing may prefer to process verbally instead. Another strategy for increasing self-awareness is participating in counseling. When students who are training to become counselors have participated in counseling as clients, they have reported higher levels of self-awareness.[29]

Self-awareness is thought to be such an important part of becoming a therapeutic person that Sigmund Freud, who is considered the first "modern psychotherapist," cautioned that therapists need to cultivate self-awareness in order to avoid transferring their own past struggles and interpretations onto their clients.[30] So, dating back to the early 1900s, self-awareness has been highly valued as a characteristic of a therapeutic person.

In addition to helping us become more therapeutic, what are some other benefits to self-awareness? Some literature suggests that as a person gets to know himself or herself, and especially as they increase in awareness of their strengths (see secret 4 for more on how to determine your signature personal strengths), they are likely to experience the following benefits:

- decreased levels of depression
- increased well-being
- higher levels of happiness
- reduced stress
- greater likelihood of achieving their goals[31]

One of the things that I learned along the journey of becoming a therapist is that sometimes things get worse before they get better. Humans have naturally created many ways of avoiding painful realities and have become experts at procrastination and avoidance. But the journey to self-awareness allows us to courageously face past hurts, unmet needs, or other emotional wounds and identify what it is that we need or needed as a function of those painful experiences. Rogers spoke of his experiences of being bullied, and it is clear that he wanted children to know that feelings could be mentioned and managed and that they can talk to people who love them about those feelings. In his response to every letter he received from a television neighbor who disclosed feelings, Rogers thanked them, let them know how glad he was they shared the feeling, and helped to provide them with whatever comfort the situation called for. He never shied away from vulnerability or painful feelings. He was aware of his own feelings and needs and could communicate them to others. He could truly share himself because *he knew himself*. Mister Rogers evoked this same knowing in others and invited them to a deeply personal place in order to be the person they needed to be so they could provide compassionate expressions of care toward themselves.

Rogers made it a priority to find out the truth about himself, and he did this so proficiently that he was able to help others by, as one friend put it, "becoming invisible" and allowing them to move to a deeper level of authenticity.[32] We can make a difference in our neighbor's white space in less than a minute of our time. One of the strategies we can use to offer more white space to neighbors may be to allow room for more pauses in conversations. We know that in the science of conversation people from all different backgrounds tend to respond in conversation within two hundred milliseconds.[33] Mister Rogers was accustomed to pacing for children, but even in interviews with adults we see he sometimes took two or even three seconds to reply. These pockets of silence can give our neighbors cognitive white space to ponder a thought a little longer or perhaps be even more present in the moment.

Another strategy is to ask questions of a conversational partner and be still in allowing responses. When a person is not anxiously shifting weight back and forth and twiddling their thumbs but rather calmly and pensively listening with interest, we feel more comfortable to open up and let our thoughts unfold. Even when

> *He was able to help others by "becoming invisible" and allowing them to move to a deeper level of authenticity.*

talking with others who were interviewing him, Rogers created some white space and paused and asked them questions.[34]

Finally, consider this:

- What would it look like for you to discover the essentials that are invisible in you?
- If you had to describe yourself to another person without using any external descriptors (appearance, job, family, etc.), how would you describe yourself?
- What does it look like to have white space in your life and to allow white space for others?

KEY TAKEAWAYS

- What is essential about any human is probably invisible to the eye.
- Everyone needs white space. Build it into your schedule.

- White space in this context means contemplation, reflection, time alone, silence, and unstructured time.

- Spending time with white space provides us with time to make sense of our experiences, which can lead to benefits such as developing personal values, forgiveness, and acceptance of what is, as well as understanding, wonderment, curiosity, spiritual pursuits, and more.

- Look past outward appearances to search for the rest of the story in each person—even yourself. Don't judge what you see on the outside.

- Have compassion for each person's inside story, even if it is painful or uncomfortable. It's okay to feel a range of emotions about it.

- We all have choices about how we'll respond to the painful parts of life.

- Be curious—about people and the world.

- Take time to process before drawing conclusions.

- Self-awareness is important in discovering the essential.

- You can increase your self-awareness through contemplative writing or participating in counseling.

A CONCEPT TO CONTEMPLATE

Take time to discover what's inside. Cultivate curiosity! Try to avoid making assumptions because what is essential about ourselves and others is invisible to the eye. In order to take a step in this direction, I invite you to consider what is essential about you that is invisible.

Show Gratitude

Be Kind and Be Thankful

The words "thank you" are probably the greatest words in any language.

Fred Rogers, in an interview with Wendy Zoba

s we covered in "A World without Mister Rogers," when Fred Rogers was to be inducted into the Television Hall of Fame, a special guest was there to surprise him with the gift of gratitude. It was—you'll recognize the name—Jeffrey Erlanger. When the lights came up and Jeffrey once again expertly maneuvered his chair to center stage, Rogers jumped out of his seat and onto the stage to hug and greet him. You could see the appreciation and joy in Rogers's eyes as he beheld his old friend and neighbor.

What was the focus of his acceptance speech? Gratitude. When Rogers took the microphone, he first paused to thank the academy and express his appreciation that they had allowed Jeffrey Erlanger to surprise him and be a part of his moment. He also shared some thoughts about the value of life and the importance of treating our neighbors well.

The audience was filled with high-profile people, as well as others Mister Rogers held dear, including his wife, Joanne. He stood next to the podium in his tuxedo, looking out from the stage and looking into the camera from behind his tortoiseshell eyeglasses. He invited the audience to ponder a rhetorical question with his oft-repeated query, "What can we do to make goodness attractive?" After pausing briefly, he did what he had made it his mission to do in each one of his speeches.

He comforted his audience, reminding them that we each have people who have loved us into becoming who we are today, those who have "helped you love the good that grows within you." He invited the audience and all watching by television to think of those who have loved them into becoming. He invited us to take a moment, ten seconds to be exact, to think of those people who loved us into becoming. He watched the time.

Many moist eyes filled the auditorium as Mister Rogers led the way in this corporate joining of strangers in mindfulness of gratitude toward those who wanted the very best for them. Those special people could be near, far, or even in heaven, he reminded us. Rogers did not stop there. There was more.

After the ten seconds of thinking of our loved ones was over, he invited us to think about how grateful those loved ones who were thought of must be that we took the time to think of them. He also made it a point to remind everyone that we have an important choice to make. He reminded us that our actions have an impact and can be used to encourage other people to do one of two things: "to demean this life, or to cherish it."[1] Mister Rogers was an advocate for appreciating and cherishing life and goodness, and seeking to make that attitude of gratitude attractive to others.

We need a bit of white space to contemplate this. Mister Rogers was a genius of gratitude! He understood the value and impact of gratitude intuitively, and appreciation was his constant companion. He closed his speech in the same way he opened it, with gratitude. He made sure to thank his colleagues in television for all the good that they do, and he made sure to thank them for also including

> *We each have people who have loved us into becoming the people we are today.*

him in that celebration. You could see gratitude in his eyes as he looked at Jeffrey Erlanger and again as he looked out into the sea of faces in the auditorium.

Principle Defined: Gratitude Equals Relationship Glue

The science of gratitude engenders hope. We know that gratitude helps us optimize the way our brains function so we bring the best of ourselves to relationships. Gratitude is relationship Miracle-Gro that keeps relationships growing and flourishing.[2]

As we've seen, a key principle from Mister Rogers's work was showing gratitude. But there are many variants of gratitude—grace, thankfulness, appreciation, and awe and wonder—that we'll discuss. *Gratitude* comes from the Latin root word *gratia*, which means *grace*.[3] The word *gratitude* conveys the idea of being on the receiving end of grace or generosity. Some experts define it as a moral affect,[4] others as an attitude,[5] some as a state of mind,[6] and still others a trait. Some scientists even look at gratitude as a two-step process: identification that a positive outcome has been obtained and recognition that the positive outcome is attributed to something or someone outside of ourselves.[7] (Thus it's both receiving and giving.) Dr. Martin Seligman, a psychologist known as the founder of positive psychology, defines gratitude as a "signature strength."[8]

For the purposes of this chapter, we will look at gratitude as a general state of mind characterized by appreciation.

Additionally, adopting a grateful state of mind allows us to give our best to ourselves and others, unlocking the following benefits:

- lower blood pressure
- enhanced immune function
- increased acts of helpfulness and generosity[9]
- increased well-being[10]
- increased life satisfaction[11]
- decreased depression[12]
- decreased risk of anxiety
- decreased risk of substance abuse disorders[13]
- quicker recovery from illness
- increased resilience[14]
- increased happiness[15]
- increased social connection[16]

- increased capacity to form and maintain relationships[17]
- increased positive relational satisfaction for self and spouse[18]

Gratitude may play an even more important role in friendships than in familial relationships.[19] Grateful people are described by others as helpful, outgoing, trustworthy, and optimistic.[20]

The Mister Rogers Effect: Wondrous Appreciation

Let's look at Mister Rogers through this lens of gratitude as a signature strength. Each day when Mister Rogers started his show, he had a song to sing, and his gratitude spilled over as he sang appreciation for the day: "It's a beautiful day in the neighborhood." He invited us to join in and become a part of his neighborhood—all of us were welcome, and he was glad that we were there. His appreciation and delight were the glue that bound all of us to the neighborhood.

Mister Rogers invited his viewers into relationship with his daily invitation "Won't you be my neighbor?" Save marriage proposals, this request—like "Will you be my valentine?"—is one of the few questions in popular discourse that proposes another person "be my" something. It is an invitation into close relationship, and it was Mister Rogers's way of opening the door to a connection and *belonging*. Many young viewers responded to this invitation by writing him letters along with their parents.

In a noisy world, Mister Rogers started each program with a song of gratitude in his heart, music to weary ears. He ended each program the same way he started it, with a song called "It's Such a Good Feeling."[21] He listed many things to be thankful for in his lyrics, including life, growth, a positive attitude, being in tune and in bloom, and lastly but perhaps most importantly, knowing that we are friends.

Mister Rogers's last show was in 2001. But in 2003, a few months before his death, Mister Rogers came out of retirement briefly and recorded one final broadcast in the WQED studio in order to say goodbye to his lifelong television neighbors. During that broadcast, he noted that he often ran into people who grew up with the neighborhood. He said they would chat for a bit and end their time with a hug. At the end of his broadcast, Mister Rogerse reminded viewers how wonderful "it is to know that we're lifelong friends."[22]

> *Mister Rogers invited his viewers into relationship with his daily invitation "Won't you be my neighbor?"*

How did he preserve this friendship and neighborly relationship with so many viewers for so long? And how did he affect so many with his life's work and touching farewell? Let's find out.

The Psychology of Gratitude

I work with a team of faculty and students to conduct research on various topics related to counseling, therapy, and personal growth (e.g., self-compassion, empathy, emotional intelligence, cognitive behavioral analysis system of psychotherapy treatment for depression, and attachment). While working on this book, our AEI (attachment and emotional intelligence) research team continuously saw the theme of Mister Rogers's grateful attitude and expressions of appreciation throughout his work. Appreciation is often an expression of admiration and fondness; the glue that holds relationships together may have been one of the many tools he used to invest in our hearts. These generous expressions of gratitude were used frequently by Mister Rogers and served to create a warm, positive emotional climate that fueled connection with his viewers. Research shows this is linked with permanence of relationship.

Mister Rogers seemed to carry with him this sense of gratitude in all his programs—indeed, in all his interactions in and out of the neighborhood. His tenure as America's beloved neighbor spanned over thirty-three years, and in each episode, he was especially good at approaching the world with awe and wonder. "So much to see, so much to see," he'd say when walking into a kindergarten classroom, as he was taking it all in for the first time. His awe and remarks about how much there was to see were subtle expressions of appreciation that modeled how to approach the world with a sense of appreciation and wonder.

What is awe? It involves three different factors: a sense of attunement to the passage of time, the gift of presence (being present in the moment with the person or persons you are with), and being tuned in to the vastness around us.[23] When Mister Rogers asked the young Jeffrey Erlanger to tell him about his experience with autonomic dysreflexia, he expressed awe and appreciation at the ten-year-old's mastery over the words *autonomic* and *dysreflexia*. Rogers often approached the world with marveling. To marvel is to find yourself lost in the wonder of the moment. Mister Rogers demonstrated how to savor each moment and how to express gratitude. Mastering marveling, awe, and wonder is a good first step in a life of appreciation and gratitude.

Developing a capacity to express appreciation, awe, and wonder can create a *positive emotional atmosphere*, which may be associated with the capacities of emotional intelligence and emotion regulation (secret 3).[24]

We've discussed some of the benefits of gratitude, but did you know it can predict longevity in your most important relationships? Dr. John Gottman has spent his life researching and analyzing relationships and has a penchant for prediction. He has been able to predict both divorce and stability of marriage with over 83 percent accuracy, and satisfaction with 80 percent accuracy. He has also developed a series of factors that predict with 94 percent accuracy whether a relationship will last. At the heart of these predictors is the idea of a mutual respect for one another and a valuing of friendship.[25] Sound familiar?

Gottman notes that if there is a high degree of mutual respect, intentional attention given to friendship, and a high number of positive interactions, then the connection between relationship partners is likely to flourish. In a vibrant and passionate relationship, these positive interactions likely fortify the relationship against stress. This buffer against negative sentiment allows couples to avoid taking offense at actions other couples may believe are a personal affront. This protection is called *positive sentiment override*—which means that if a person is running late, you assume they tried to get there on time but must be caught in traffic or in some other attribution beyond their control. You assume the best motives. With negative sentiment override, running late would be interpreted as an affront, accompanied by negative feelings bubbling up into awareness. For example, "He is so inconsiderate, he is always late." Or, "He just does not value my time at all!"

Although Dr. Gottman originally focused his research on couples, other psychological researchers have applied his work to many other types of interpersonal relationships. Some researchers have found that many of the same principles hold true for relationships between adolescent girls and their mothers.[26] Other researchers have applied Gottman's approach to professional relationships, and it has been applied to connections between student doctors' emotional exchanges with their patients.[27] We know that as levels of gratitude go up, levels of loneliness tend to decrease, and gratitude promotes social bonding.[28]

This is an important concept for parents, teachers, and anyone in a helping profession. Gratitude affects everything.

For relationships to make it for the long haul, research reveals the number of positive interactions needs to be greater than the number of negative interactions—specifically about five times as great. So for every negative interaction, there need to be at least five positives to create an overall atmosphere of emotional positivity.[29] Each time Mister Rogers reminded us with the words "You have made today a special day, just by your being you," he was expressing appreciation and adding to that day's number of positive interactions, creating a positive emotional atmosphere.

In Gottman's studies, he demonstrated that relationships need fondness and admiration to last; we must look for the positive in others and express it. *Admiration* is a synonym for *appreciation*,[30] and Mister Rogers used it liberally to make a connection with his viewers and to help them feel appreciated and special.

On the other hand, there is one emotion that erodes love. According to Gottman's research, contempt erodes love faster than anything else. What is the cure? The close companions of gratitude—fondness and admiration. Gottman notes that even in relationships where admiration for each other has waned, it can still be revived with the power of appreciation. He encourages couples to begin looking for what they appreciate in their partners.

> In such a case the key to reinvigorating fondness and admiration is to get in the habit of scanning for qualities and actions that you can appreciate. And then let your partner know what you've observed and are *grateful* for. These everyday thank-you's don't have to be about momentous acts on your spouse's part. Catch your partner doing some little thing right and then offer a genuine appreciation like, "I love the way you handled the teacher conference yesterday."[31] (emphasis added)

Mister Rogers modeled this well; he was often scanning for qualities (in people) and wonderment (in the world) to catch and appreciate. It was his lifelong habit. Scanning our environment in a positive way involves maintaining a sense of wonder while curiously seeking out what we can appreciate. For example, one day Rogers walked into his television living room and announced, "I've been thinking about zippers!" and then he invited us on a field trip to a zipper factory to learn how they were made.[32]

He also "caught" people doing something right. For example, he caught Jeffrey Erlanger maneuvering his chair well, and he caught the kindergarten classroom having so much to see. Rogers told Charlie Rose that he found that the act of being a gracious receiver was also a wonderful gift to give[33]—something we should all remember. Mister Rogers was an expert catcher of good things.

We tend to find what we are looking for. Ever shop for a new car, or a new used car? I remember looking for a Toyota Corolla in graduate school. All of a sudden, Corollas were everywhere! I guess they had been there

> *He inhaled wonder and exhaled appreciation. We can too.*

all along, but I was suddenly noticing them. Mister Rogers was on the lookout for good things—*and he found them.* He inhaled wonder and exhaled appreciation. We can too.

Gratitude's Ripple Effect

Gratitude is associated with a host of benefits for individuals and those we are in relationship with. It is like a gift that keeps on giving. Likewise, when we hold on to gratitude without giving it away, it's like holding on to a beautifully wrapped present and letting it sit in the corner and collect dust while the intended recipient wonders if you forgot their birthday and you feel guilty for letting it sit.

Not only does gratitude make the grateful person happier, healthier, and more successful, but it also impacts those *around* them positively. A Taiwanese research team examined the role of husbands' expressions of happiness on the depression levels of their wives. The researchers found that there is indeed a link between a man's expression of gratitude and his wife's depression level. As a husband's dispositional gratitude increased, his wife's depressive emotion decreased![34]

This research suggests that it is helpful not only to cultivate gratitude in oneself but also to live with and among others who cultivate gratitude.

Gratitude is beneficial for relationships and connection. When people are grateful, their peers tend to rate their behavior more favorably and consider them to be more prosocial. Gratitude impacts relationships by making them stronger and more stable. In a world where we may be both loved and wounded by those close to us, the healing balm of gratitude is crucial.

Not only does gratitude make the grateful person happier, healthier, and more successful, but it also impacts those around them positively.

This is reminiscent of a quote that is attributed to psychologist Ben Sweetland: "We cannot hold a torch to light another's path without brightening our own." The motivation behind expressing gratitude may be to make another person feel appreciated, but it tends to make the other person think more of you, feel closer and more connected to you, and potentially make the other person have a sense that their relationship with you is more stable and secure.

Using the Gratitude Secret in Your Own Neighborhood

What is it like to feel gratitude? This may be different for each of us, particularly since there are so many elements of gratitude: grace and thankfulness, awe and wonder, fondness and admiration, giving and receiving. Ultimately, it is what binds human relationships, so cultivating gratitude matters.

Here's a list of action items to help you begin experiencing the benefits of gratitude!

- One oft-used method is to journal what you are thankful for. Some families use a dinnertime "praise report" to enumerate the good that happened during the day. Whether written or spoken, counting one's blessings can have a surprising effect.

- Additionally, take some time and white space to savor life; think of the little blessings as gifts and take a moment to relish them. Recognizing that sometimes less is more, leave more margin in your schedule and daily routine so you have more time to enjoy the little moments and the simple treasures. If you would like an extra dose of motivation and a structured approach, try a daily gratitude journaling exercise, a T-list. This practice has been associated with a host of benefits, including "higher reported levels of the positive states of alertness, enthusiasm, determination, attentiveness, and energy."[35]

- Reflect on those who have "loved you into becoming," whether they are close to you geographically, far away, or even in heaven, as Rogers would say.

- Consider reading *Authentic Happiness* by Martin Seligman and *The World According to Mister Rogers* by Fred Rogers.

- Identify your signature strengths! Visit the Authentic Happiness website to complete the signature strengths assessment and identify your signature strengths.[36] Then take a moment to appreciate your makeup and the strengths that lie within you.

- Take a moment to think about someone in your life that you are thankful for and consider having what Rogers would call a "letter visit" with them: send them a thank-you card. Dr. Seligman suggests in-person letter visits when possible, where you laminate a letter and take it on a visit to the person but keep the purpose vague and surprise them. Then leave the laminated letter with them as a gift.

- Consider purchasing a box of thank-you notes or make your own and begin sending thank-yous out each time someone does something you appreciate or just to let them know you appreciate their friendship.

- Think of one thing you could do today that your future self would thank you for. Consider doing that.

KEY TAKEAWAYS

- Grateful people tend to have better relationships. Gratitude equals relationship glue.

- There are many elements of gratitude: grace, thankfulness, appreciation, awe, wonderment, fondness, admiration. It is both giving and receiving.

- Possessing an attitude of gratitude has many benefits, including lower blood pressure, enhanced immune function, decreased depression, and increased resilience.

- Practicing gratitude increases one's sense of well-being and happiness.

- Mastering awe and wonderment is a good first step toward a life of appreciation and gratitude.

- To make relationships flourish, we must look for the positive in others and our experiences with them and express our appreciation.

- If you are on the lookout for good things, you will find them.

- Feeling and expressing gratitude may be different for each individual. Start somewhere.

A CONCEPT TO CONTEMPLATE

Be kind and be thankful for everything. Approach the world with awe and wonder—and remember gratitude improves every relationship.

In this moment, what are you grateful for? Consider expressing it. Everyone likes getting a thank-you note.

Develop Empathy

Be with People Where They Are

There isn't anyone you couldn't love once you've heard their story.

Sister Mary Lou Kownacki, director,
Monasteries of the Heart

*I*t was 1985 and Mister Rogers was appearing as a guest on a talk show that had been rated number one season after season. It was the *Oprah Winfrey Show*. Rogers, known for turning interviews around on his interviewers, was about to defy expectations, giving more answers than questions to a very important question.

Oprah walked toward Mister Rogers wearing her bold red lipstick, arms tightly folded over her chest. "What do you think is the biggest mistake parents make in raising their children?" she asked.

Anticipation filled the air for a moment as Rogers took a deep breath, gazed toward the floor, and finally looked up. "Not to remember their own childhood," he answered as a knowing smile spread across his face.

Mister Rogers seemed to be calling parents to remember an important secret—empathy—which allows us to relate to children as we remember what our own childhoods were like.

He looked at Oprah for a moment. "Yeah," she said quietly. Rogers nodded and continued. "I think that the best thing we can do is to think about what it was like for us and know what our children are going through."

Oprah quickly responded, "But you know what, it's so hard."

As she spoke, I wondered if she was empathizing with the parent and Rogers with the child. Oprah continued, explaining the challenges of adulthood and how we may vow to do things differently and not put our children through the things that bothered us: "You say, 'I will never do this' when your mother's doing it to you or your father's doing it to you. You always say, 'I will never do this to my child.'"

Rogers nodded politely and murmured a supportive "Mm-hmm."

With this implied encouragement, Oprah got even more animated. "And you forget what it is like to be this size!" she said, indicating some children in the audience. "You really do forget."

Rogers again nodded supportively and then said, "But those children can help re-evoke what it was like, and that's why when you're a parent, you have a new chance to grow."[1]

Watching this interview years later, I could not help but smile at these words, knowing that Rogers was once again teaching us about empathy. He seemed to be encouraging parents who were watching Oprah's show to *lean into their discomfort* and find a new opportunity to grow by remembering their own childhoods and having empathy for their own children. This, he must have thought, would make them better parents.

What Empathy Is . . . and Isn't

Many definitions exist for empathy. Perhaps the most basic is the classic metaphor of walking a mile in another person's shoes. But there's more to it than that. True empathy feels what another feels from *their* frame of reference—actually understanding their story and feeling what they feel, sensing what it is like to walk around in their world.

But empathy can easily elude us. If I look at Joe's choices, I may find myself saying, "If I were him, I would not do that." Of course, I wouldn't—I'm not Joe. Empathy requires truly adventuring into and walking around in Joe's world so that I might be able to understand him better.

In other words, empathy involves seeking to experience the world as others do. Empathy also requires courageously being willing to be vulnerable and connect to a similar feeling in ourselves. For example, if

> *Empathy requires courageously being willing to be vulnerable and connect to a similar feeling in ourselves.*

my friend tells me that her beloved pet cat has died, then I may have to go within myself to remember the pain of losing my own pet without getting lost in preoccupation. As I connect with the pain of the loss, I can move toward a more cognitive empathy and think about how my friend may be experiencing that pain.

Psychologists parse this definition a bit further, breaking it into cognitive (thought) empathy and affective (feeling) empathy. Cognitive empathy is simply the ability to understand another's perspective, while affective empathy is the ability to respond to another's emotional state with a corresponding emotion of our own.

True empathy also has a few prerequisites. When exercising empathy, we use courage to step into another's frame of reference and vulnerably connect with both their thoughts and their feelings. We demonstrate that empathy involves giving those feelings and thoughts a voice and capturing the essence of the other's perspective. It is experiential.

However, empathy is not the same as sympathy. In two words, empathy can be thought of as *feeling with*, while sympathy means *feeling for*. The subtle distinction between empathy and its close cousin sympathy can escape even trained students of psychology. Empathy looks at you as if looking through your eyes and into your tired heart. Empathy, like the friend that nourishes your soul with homemade soup on a cold winter day, says, "Ah, I can sense the stress you are feeling on top of being sick and the tension you are carrying. It sounds like you have been working very hard." On the other hand, sympathy may express herself as the friend who is slightly annoyed to have to hear about your struggle. She is compelled to engage in condescending one-upmanship and may say something like, "Aw, I'm sorry you have been having so many headaches lately. I had a migraine yesterday. That must really suck for you."

In class, when I initially ask for examples of empathetic statements, students often instinctively offer, "I am sorry for your loss." This is not empathy but rather an expression of sympathy. It generally shuts down the connection and garners a simple thank-you in response. Period—end of discussion.

Meanwhile, the conversation expander, empathy, seeks to connect experientially with the thoughts and feelings of the other person, as would be the case if one said, "Oh, I was saddened to hear about your grandmother. I know you were very close to her and that you emailed each other often. It must be really hard to lose someone who was so important to you. You must really miss her." Empathy requires a deeper level of understanding and connection with human emotions, which enables one to engage with others in a more meaningful way.

Empathy's embrace is the warm hug and the shoulder we may cry on. (Although it's important to remember that even though we think of empathy as feeling someone's pain, we can feel their joy too.) It is easy to spot Mister Rogers's empathy in all aspects of his programs; it's woven into every scene.

The Mister Rogers Effect: Empathy

Let's look at how Mister Rogers taught kids about empathy in a program that aired in 1981.[2] Mister Rogers was in the middle of showing viewers some paper cups when his delivery man and friend Mr. McFeely stopped by. But that day he didn't have one of his customary speedy deliveries. Rather, Mr. McFeely held a ragged sheet of music. Rogers sat down next to McFeely on the piano bench to play the music, which turned out to be a love song. It reminded Mr. McFeely of his wedding.

Mister Rogers and Mr. McFeely talked about the wedding; we even saw the vows in a flashback. Rogers asked McFeely if he had always been happy in his marriage, and McFeely explained that no one can always be happy but that he and his wife had their share of happiness.

"Well, some people get married, and after a while they're so unhappy with each other that they don't want to be married anymore," Mister Rogers said. And suddenly, something changed. Mr. McFeely's eyes shifted downward, he squirmed on the piano bench, and with pressured speech he said, "I know and sometimes they get divorced, and that's all very sad." Then he snatched his scrap of paper with the music on it, muttered about how he must be going right away, and hustled to the door. Mister Rogers appeared unaffected by Mr. McFeely's speedy departure. He simply thanked him for telling us about his wedding.

Mister Rogers returned to the kitchen and the cups, as he reflected on this experience with Mr. McFeely. He said, "Mr. McFeely left so fast—as soon as we started talking about divorce." He so casually talked about the elephant in the room! As an adult watching this familiar scene again, I marvel at how good Rogers was. He expressed empathy for Mr. McFeely, giving voice to the seemingly obvious and confirming our suspicions: "I guess he doesn't like to talk about it."

Rogers helped us to empathize with Mr. McFeely. His simple approach to the topic made us think, "I wonder what happened to Mr. McFeely in his childhood. Could he be running away from some of his own thoughts and feelings, rather than running away from Mister Rogers?"

As Rogers sat back down at the table with the cups, we were drawn in as he asked us whether we knew someone who had been divorced. Then he comforted us with these words: "Well, [divorce] is something we *can* talk about." And he invited us to join in to "something important." He validated our feelings and gave us permission to talk about something we might have been afraid to talk about. He went on to share a story about both a boy and a girl whose parents happened to get divorced and they thought it was all their fault, so they cried and cried. Though, Rogers assured us, it was not their fault.

Next thing we knew, we were off to a picnic in the Land of Make Believe, but we were not going there to escape reality. We were going *to use imagination to find a way to talk about* divorce that allowed for creativity and expression. Once we were immersed in the Land of Make Believe, a single mom and little girl came by for a visit. As the little girl and Prince Tuesday got to know one another, Tuesday asked where the girl's daddy was. She explained that her parents were divorced, and they did not love each other anymore (though they both loved her). Prince Tuesday showed empathy for her. He reiterated that they did not love each other anymore, and he empathized about how terrible it must feel. His newfound friend assured him that it only felt awful sometimes. Moments later we were transported back to the kitchen table, picking up with our important chat.

Rogers asked us if we noticed that the little girl knew her parents still loved her. Then he asked us how we thought Prince Tuesday felt about this chat about divorce. Here

Rogers was teaching us about empathy. We had to consider what this talk felt like to us and how it might have felt for Tuesday. So much for one-way conversations on television. As per usual, Rogers definitely pulled us into this discussion on divorce, giving us many points to ponder.

Mister Rogers spoke slowly. Looking into the camera, he paused and allowed each statement to sink in. In one brief segment of this thirty-minute program, he taught six important lessons about empathy.

1. Sometimes other people do not like to talk about topics like divorce, and that is okay. We can have empathy for their preferences (thought empathy).
2. Remember your QTIP (do not take another person's discomfort personally).
3. Express appreciation for what someone is willing to disclose and seek to understand how difficult it could be for them to elaborate (thought and feeling empathy, as Rogers demonstrated with McFeely).
4. Talking about divorce may be difficult, but it is possible (thought empathy).
5. Avoid blaming yourself for other people's actions. It is not your fault if your parents get divorced (self-empathy; having compassionate talk toward yourself).
6. Feelings are mentionable and manageable. It's good to be interested in and to identify the feelings of others (thought and feeling empathy).

These lessons in empathy help make it possible to connect with others emotionally and to be emotionally available. This demonstration of empathy was not a one-off for Rogers. He considered the needs and feelings of his viewers and let them inform his programming in important ways. For example, he once received a letter from a little girl named Katie who was blind. Her blindness did not stop her from following and listening to *Mister Rogers' Neighborhood*. In her letter, Katie shared her concern about Mister Rogers's fish. She could not see if Mister Rogers was feeding the fish in the tank in his television home. In her letter she kindly and politely asked, "Please say when you are feeding your fish, because I worry about them. I can't see if you are feeding them, so please say you are feeding them out loud."[3]

From then on, Mister Rogers always took special care to announce when he was feeding the fish. He expressed empathy and concern for his neighbors not only through his words but also in his actions and commitments. He continued doing this, probably long after Katie outgrew the neighborhood program.

> *He expressed empathy and concern for his neighbors not only through his words but also in his actions and commitments.*

The impact of Mister Rogers's acts of kindness did not end with Katie. In February 2018, pop-culture figure Chrissy Teigen tweeted, "Mister Rogers would narrate himself feeding the fish each episode with 'I'm feeding the fish' because of a letter he received from a young blind girl [Katie] who was worried the fish were hungry. Love you, Mister Rogers." As of August 19, 2019, Chrissy Teigen's post was retweeted 30,728 times and liked 175,579 times and counting.[4]

Through social media, online archives, movies, and television, Rogers's kind spirit and empathetic actions still move the hearts of Americans today. Radical empathy allowed Rogers to connect with a broad and diverse range of people, and his emotional intelligence helped him to regulate himself and continue expressing empathy in situations where many people would likely become defensive.

The Psychology of Empathy

Empathy is vital in times of trouble, loss, and trauma, but it has benefits in everyday human interactions as well. For example, one of the laws that governs human behavior is the law of reciprocity, which can lead to an increase or decrease in cooperation, depending upon the initiator's actions. You could call reciprocity "tit for tat." However, the tit-for-tat approach is reactive. For example, if a friend does not call to initiate getting together for coffee despite saying, "Hey, we should get together sometime," then you might say to yourself, "Well, she has not contacted me, so I will not contact her."

In some situations, this can lead to an increase in noncooperative behavior and/or conflict. Relationship researchers have found that when one person criticizes another, the verbal attack elicits defensiveness and a counterattack. Here's an example:

Wife: "You never call when you are running late." (never = criticism, making a complaint into an absolute, continual characteristic)

Husband: "My phone was in the back seat and I could not reach it." (defensive response) "Why do you always get so easily frustrated? You need to relax." (countercriticism)

If this tit-for-tat approach continues, the conflict can escalate. But slight modifications, such as engaging in emotional generosity (empathy), can decrease noncooperative behavior:

Wife: "You never call when you are running late."

Husband: "I know you have been under a lot of stress with hosting this party. It must have been frustrating that you were waiting for me to bring the ingredients from the grocery to finish cooking." (sees past the criticism and expresses compassion = emotional generosity, expression of empathy)

"I left my phone in the back seat and could not reach it to call you. I thought pulling over to call would delay me more."

Wife: "Well, okay. I guess it is better late than never. Thank you."

You can easily see how generosity, when added to a tit-for-tat interaction, can lead to more cooperation and positive social behavior. Cooperation is one benefit of the manifestation of empathy.[5] But there are others.

Researchers found a number of different benefits associated with empathy, including

- increased positive social behavior;
- decreased noncooperative behavior;

- increased willingness to help others without reciprocation or long-term benefits for oneself;
- facilitated kindness;[6]
- enhanced moral courage;[7]
- an effective remedy for and safeguard against bullying;
- predicted altruism;[8]
- more successful relationships;[9]
- provision of emotional support; and
- higher relationship satisfaction.[10]

Additionally, adolescents who are empathetic tend to be more willing to accept parental control.[11] Empathy in children may also predict the probability that they will jump in and intervene to defend victims of sexual assault.[12] Exercising empathy can activate our brain's reward system and impact dopamine levels, resulting in a sense of physiological reward.[13]

Empathy can also have some surprising uses. For example, Chris Voss, a former FBI hostage negotiator, revealed that empathy can be helpful in hostage negotiations. The process he used is what the FBI calls *labeling*.[14]

The FBI's labeling process involves the same skill set counselors use. They identify feelings that are likely to be associated with the circumstances and give the hostage takers' feelings a voice by stating their feelings aloud, thus reflecting their feelings back to them. This is not unlike what therapists do. It's the same thing Mister Rogers did with his program on divorce.

Empathy or compassion directed toward oneself is also associated with a host of benefits, such as

- decreased inclination to see the worst in others as a strategy for rating oneself more favorably;[15]
- the tendency to feel more compassion toward others;
- emotional intelligence involving an openness to one's own suffering and a tendency to respond with kindness; and
- respect for oneself and an increased likelihood to forgive one's own mistakes as actions of a fallible and imperfect human being.[16]

When empathy is sewn into partner communication, it leads to a stronger bond between relationship partners and opens the door for continued positive interactions.

Demonstrating and communicating with empathy is the healthy relational glue that helps us stick together in kind and cooperative relationships. Imago therapists, who practice a type of therapy that emerged in the 1980s, focus on helping couples heal the inner child in themselves and one another, using the tools of empathy and connection. The belief among therapists in the power of empathy is so prominent that one of the antidotes they use to heal problems in couple relations is the development of empathy. Knowing this, we can seek to enhance empathy in ourselves, our children, those we teach or mentor, and so on.

Demonstrating and communicating with empathy is the healthy relational glue that helps us stick together in kind and cooperative relationships.

Not only does empathy play a role in positive behaviors, cooperation, kindness in interpersonal relationships, and decreased cruelty but it also has academic implications. Researchers have even found that statistical tools can be used to predict future success in some academic areas based on empathy. Some of these academic skills that empathy has the power to forecast include critical thinking, math, and reading.[17] The empathetic Mister Rogers modeled empathy for us in every carefully curated episode. We have many reasons to comfort our neighbors and loved ones with empathy. However altruistic and neighborly it may be to wear our empathetic hats, this state of mind may benefit us as well. It may even open the door to a cozier and happier life.

Empathy, Happiness, and Hygge

Empathy plays an important role in human happiness. It starts with the principle of reciprocity as it's experienced early in life. A baby smiles and his mother smiles back at him—and the baby smiles again. As children grow, they learn empathy in other ways; for example, a hug and warm words of encouragement when they fall off their bike provide empathy from a loving adult. Empathy, as we've noted, promotes relationships. If you fail to learn empathy, relationships with others include less love, and without that, it's difficult to find fulfillment.

The good news is empathy can be taught.[18]

According to the World Happiness Report, Denmark has been ranked among the top three happiest countries in the world for the past seven years and counting.[19] Empathy is considered a central component of the educational agenda in Denmark, and it is credited in part for their high happiness ranking.[20] Kindergarten to high school–age students participate in empathy lessons, deemed as necessary as math class. Clearly Danish educators value the role empathy plays in child development.

The Danish school curriculum includes one hour of *Klassens tid* (Danish for "class time") each week that is dedicated to working on empathy. Beginning as early as age six and lasting for about a decade, Klassens tid teaches students how to help each other rather than compete with one another.[21] There is also a program that gives children under the age of six the opportunity to view pictures of peers displaying a range of emotions including fear, sadness, and anger. At an early age, they learn to identify emotions in themselves and others in a mindful manner. They learn to accept emotions without judgment and to demonstrate empathy![22]

In elementary school, the hour-long class includes time for students to share struggles or problems that they are faced with, and collectively, the whole class including the teacher, rallies together to participate in finding a solution using their listening skills (see secret 1).

On days when there are no problems to discuss, the focus shifts to experiencing *hygge* together. (The word sounds like "who-ga.") Hygge is the Danish secret to a warm and cozy thriving nation, despite the light variations associated with their northern climate. Hygge finds its origins in a Norwegian word that means "well-being" and has been described as creating intimacy with intentionality. The term encompasses the ideas represented by English words like *coziness, comfort, contentment*, and *companionship*.[23] When we share these feelings with others, the joyful version of empathy is stimulated.

The concept of hygge involves togetherness and warmth. There is an emphasis on sharing the spotlight and/or sharing good food (perhaps a homemade soup with made-from-scratch bread). As we've noted, this capacity to consider the stories, needs, and feelings of others involves empathy. The hygge manifesto includes several key components, such as

- atmosphere (think lamps and candles);
- being present (taking time to disconnect from media and phones);
- pleasure (eating good food);
- harmony (taking an interest in your neighbor rather than only your own experiences);
- comfort (think soft cardigan sweaters);
- truce (focusing more on connecting and not spending time arguing over things like politics);
- togetherness (building memories); and
- shelter (or a sense of community and belonging).[24]

We could all benefit from learning more about happiness and empathy from the concept of hygge. I think Mister Rogers brought it to us through his empathy before we even understood what it was.

Using the Empathy Secret in Your Own Neighborhood

If you have ever flown on an airplane, you have heard the flight attendants discuss what to do in case of an emergency. They remind passengers that it is important to put on your own oxygen mask before helping other passengers.

What does it mean to put on your own oxygen mask in the case of empathy? It means to be compassionate toward yourself before exercising empathy with others. Replacing the internal critic with a compassionate, kind friend can be transformational. I remember when my dear friend Rebekah told me how she coped during a difficult transition: "I realized that I had to become my own best friend and enjoy my own company, and so I did."

How do you talk to yourself? Like a dear friend or a harsh critic? Herein lies the first step to becoming empathetic toward ourselves. Thoughts such as "What is wrong with you? Why aren't you more productive? More attractive? Stronger?" can leave us feeling like a prisoner to the sentencing of a harsh judge. However, if we speak to ourselves as a kind friend or loved one, we become a compassionate friend to ourselves—the first step in being able to bring that same compassion to others in our neighborhoods.

Next we must develop an awareness of the subtle distinction between empathy and sympathy. It can be easy to miss, and if we do, we inadvertently shut down a conversation rather than create an empathetic connection.

Consider the responses in the table below. If you can hear yourself using phrases in column one, try experimenting with some of the phrases in column two to enhance your communication of empathy in your dialogue with friends, loved ones, students, children, and those that you help. Remember that people are different, and part of being empathetic involves staying tuned in to the individual and trying to determine which response fits best. These are not one size fits all.

As a helper, consider encouraging children to choose empathy over sympathy when possible.

Common Sympathy Response	Enhanced Empathy Response
I am so sorry your dog died.	I remember you sharing you had your dog for fifteen years. It must hurt to lose such an important part of your family. OR Language such as: "Aw, that hurts." OR Attentive silence marked with compassionate nonverbal facial expressions..
Don't cry. It's okay.	It is okay to cry. I am here to be with you. OR If the tears had words, what would they say?
(In response to someone talking about their bad day.) Well, just try not to think about it, and try to be positive.	It sounds like that was so stressful, what helped you make it through the workday? OR Help me understand more about the stress.
(In response to, "My boyfriend and I have been in conflict a lot lately.") Aw, that sucks.	Conflict can be so tiring. Help me understand more about what you think is triggering the disagreement.
(In response to someone getting demoted at work.) Well, at least you still have a job.	It must be _____ (fill in the blank with probable feeling: frustrating, hurtful, disappointing) to experience this after working so hard for so long. OR Tell me more about how you feel.
(In response to, "I have felt so tired lately.") Well, what are you doing about that? OR Maybe you should drink some coffee. OR You are tired? I have been exhausted!	Aw, it sounds like you have been working so hard lately and feeling in need of some rest. Tell me more.

Whether you are a parent, teacher, grandparent, mentor, counselor, or social worker, you can help people of all ages develop empathy and thus become more emotionally available to their neighbors. Here are some sample questions and statements for cultivating empathetic dialogue.

- How do you think (insert name) is feeling after having this conversation?
- (Insert name) may be (insert feeling) because (insert reason). E.g., Joe may be worried because he just learned about his parents' divorce.
- How would you feel if (insert scenario of another child's painful situation) happened to you?
- "I have to remember my QTIP and quit taking it personally when (insert name) changes the subject when I share my feelings. I guess he does not like talking about feelings." (We will talk more about acceptance in the next chapter).

KEY TAKEAWAYS

- True empathy feels what another feels from *their* frame of reference—actually understanding their story and feeling what they feel about it.
- There are two types of empathy: cognitive (thought) empathy and affective (feeling) empathy.
- Thought empathy is an ability to understand another's perspective, while feeling empathy is the ability to respond to another's emotional state with a corresponding emotion.

- Empathy is not the same as sympathy. Empathy feels *with*; sympathy feels *for*.
- Even though we think of empathy as feeling someone's pain, we can feel their joy too.
- Sometimes other people do not like to talk about unpleasant topics, and that is okay. We can have empathy for their preferences.
- Empathy is vital in times of trouble, loss, and trauma, and its benefits extend to everyday interactions as well.
- Empathy can be expressed in many different ways, including but not limited to generosity, compassion, kindness, vulnerability, altruism, happiness, validation, thankfulness, positivity, understanding, sharing, appreciation, warmth, rapport, tenderness, perceptiveness, grace, affection, communication, encouragement, relationship, listening, being present, and comfort.
- Being empathetic toward yourself makes you more capable of exercising empathy with others.

A CONCEPT TO CONTEMPLATE

Be with people where they really are. Put yourself in their place and feel what they feel, even their messy emotions. Empathy makes every relationship better. A first step may be to do the following: write down how you could express empathy (rather than sympathy) toward a friend or loved one who is hurting.

Practice Acceptance

Who You Are Right Now Is Acceptable

When we love a person, we accept him or her exactly as is: the lovely with the unlovely, the strong with the fearful, the true mixed in with the facade, and of course, the only way we can do it is by accepting ourselves that way.

Fred Rogers, *The World According to Mister Rogers*

*M*ercy stood on her tippy toes in the kitchen, gazing at her mother's beauty and admiring her skill as she began chopping vegetables and preparing the evening meal. The inquisitive four-year-old asked questions about everything her mother was doing. She was taken in by the vibrant orange color of the vegetables her mother prepared: "What are you cutting?"

Her mother replied, "Carrots. They are good for keeping your skin and eyes healthy." More questions flowed from Mercy, and the two chatted. Patiently and lovingly her mother answered, and they enjoyed their time together.

Then it happened. Everything changed. The front door swung open and slammed shut with a loud bang, and he came into the kitchen. "GET THE HELL OUT OF HERE NOW!" he screamed at Mercy. She caught a glimpse of his eyes and saw so much anger and hatred that she froze, her little body trembling. "I SAID GET!" Now even more irate, he swung his arm to hit her. But he hit the air—she was gone. Mercy ran upstairs into a lonely room on the other end of the house. She jumped into the bed and pulled the covers over her head. Her body heaved as she silently sobbed, not daring to make a sound—lest it rouse further wrath.

Mercy cried the tears of a terrified child who had no idea what she'd done to bring this anger down around her. She wished she could disappear; she wished for no more yelling. She had been spoken to harshly; she'd been hit, slapped, shaken, and smashed into a wall. Just a little four-year-old. Mercy buried her face in her big stuffed bunny; then, in search of something to escape loneliness and fear, she picked up the remote and turned on the TV.

Over her quiet sobs, she heard a kind man talking. She raised her head from her stuffed rabbit and locked eyes with him. It was as if he was looking right at Mercy. He had such kind eyes, so full of care and concern, that she felt a flutter of life deep within her. It was a feeling of hope mingled with comfort.

His caring voice filled her ears and soothed her. Where did he come from? Was he an angel? She remembered her grandpa teaching her about guardian angels. Perhaps her angel had come at last. The man on TV entered the front door of a television house, and he sang straight to her broken heart, "It's a beautiful day . . . won't you be mine? Won't you be my neighbor?"

Mercy had never met a man like this. Her tears stopped, and her heart swelled with each word he said. "Could this be true?" she wondered. Could this kind man like her? She watched as he calmly and rhythmically changed into a sweater and comfortable shoes.

She had seen this program before, but this time felt different. Her heart sang, "YES! YES! I will be your neighbor!" She closed her eyes when the program ended; she could still see Mister Rogers's face, his kind eyes, and his red sweater. She relished the comfort she had found in the sound of his gentle voice and those kind eyes, replaying his words again and again.

From that time on, when her father screamed, "Get out!" Mercy would retreat to her vision of Mister Rogers. Whenever she had a chance, she looked for him on TV. She loved how he always greeted her with a smile and an invitation to be his neighbor.

Years later, sitting in my counseling office, a twenty-five-year-old Mercy, eyes brimming with tears, recalled this refuge of hope. After our discussion, she realized that with her unstable family background (her mother retreated from the abuse into alcoholism) and the trauma she'd endured, Mister Rogers's dependable routine (changing his sweater and shoes, for example) and steady kindness helped her feel safe and comforted. She had longed for this safety, and it still comforted her to know that this kindness existed. Her father's anger might have bruised her body, but he could not destroy her heart.

Yes, there are people like Mister Rogers in the world, Mercy learned, and she looked for them. This knowledge gave her courage to face another day of whatever came her way. It restored her hope. Mister Rogers's kind message became a steel wall around her heart, a refuge of safety where she would often retreat. She would run to her room and cry, and in her heart, she would see his face and hear his words: "There is no one in the world like you, and I like you just the way you are." No words of hatred and cruelty would hurt her in that refuge, and her face would not be darkened with shame.

Looking back on her past with *Mister Rogers' Neighborhood*, Mercy said, "I felt *accepted*, safe; I felt like I belonged. Instead of yelling at me to get out, he was singing to me, inviting me to be his neighbor. If this kind man accepted and wanted me and believed it was a beautiful day and I was special, then I could get up to face another day. People sometimes say that a person saved their life and refer to them as a life saver. Well, Mister Rogers was not only a life saver for me. Mister Rogers was a heart saver, because he accepted and saved my wounded heart."

In our counseling session, Mercy had an epiphany about her work as a teaching missionary. She taught English to children at orphanages in Russia and El Salvador. "I internalized the structure, the stability, the kind eyes," she said. She taught her students Mister Rogers's introductory song, "It's a Beautiful Day in the Neighborhood." At the end of every mission, she left each orphan with the words that had saved her heart: "Always remember, there is no one else in the world like you, and I like you just the way you are."

"If I had not gone through the pain, experienced Rogers's acceptance, and healed," Mercy added, "then I would not be here teaching children and helping them know that they are special and accepted too. It is all part of my story. I accept the good with the bad and know it has made me who I am."

The Origins of the Acceptance Message

Rogers wove a message through all his programs reminding us that we are special and that we have made the day a special day just by being ourselves. Rogers had often heard, "Freddy, you have made today a special day, and I'm glad you're here!" from his grandpa, Fred Brooks McFeely, and those words taught him *the secret of acceptance.*[1]

There are two important dimensions of acceptance: self-acceptance and other-acceptance. Of course, as the quote at the start of this chapter indicates, Mister Rogers believed that self-acceptance was a prerequisite to other-acceptance. Self-acceptance is defined by famous therapist and founder of rational emotive behavioral therapy, Dr. Albert Ellis, as *unconditional acceptance of the self*, regardless of whether we live up to our expectations.[2] Self-acceptance involves accepting oneself unconditionally as having inherent worth, despite the inevitable imperfections that come with being human. This attitude toward ourselves has been called different things: self-empathy, self-compassion, and self-acceptance.

It differs from self-esteem, in that self-esteem looks at the extent to which one accepts himself or herself to determine feelings of self-worth. Research shows that low levels of self-acceptance and self-esteem seem to be linked to psychological ills that include depression and anxiety.[3]

The value of acceptance extends to others. But self-acceptance is required for other-acceptance, so we must start there. That said, acceptance of others is crucial to our mental and emotional health. Mister Rogers not only modeled self-acceptance but also demonstrated radical acceptance of others. For example, he stopped production of a show because someone on staff said to a puppet, "Don't cry." He let them know that they were never to tell a child, an adult, or even a puppet not to cry.[4] Instead his philosophy taught that we should *be with* and *feel with* others (secret 5) while they express tears or any unpleasant emotions (secret 2), which shows we accept others as they are.

> *Mister Rogers not only modeled self-acceptance but also demonstrated radical acceptance of others.*

The Mister Rogers Effect: Accepting Others

Mister Rogers modeled the importance of accepting ourselves so that we can be free to become who we really are. For example, in one episode he was demonstrating how to draw a picture of a house. He started to criticize himself for his lack of drawing skills, but then he stopped. It didn't matter, he said. "It's just the fun of doing it that's important!"[5]

But this message of acceptance was not limited to young children. Rogers was often invited to speak at commencement ceremonies at institutions such as Boston University, Dartmouth College, and Marquette University. His address at Dartmouth was a memorable one, and yet his message of acceptance remained the same. Here he brought acceptance to the public square and gave it a microphone.

> It's not the honors and the prizes and the fancy outsides of life which ultimately nourish our souls; it is the knowing that we can be trusted, that we never have to fear the truth, that the bedrock of our lives, from which we make our choices, is very good stuff. There is a neighborhood song that is meant for the child in each of us. "It's You I Like."[6]

Rogers went on to recite the words to "It's You I Like," reminding the audience that it isn't the accomplishments or the things, like Ivy League degrees, that represent us. Rather it's the invisible that really matters (secret 3). He reminded the new grads that they can be loved regardless of what they do—just by being themselves.

Rogers was always listening to and reading people (secret 1). He was always seeking to meet and be with them right where they really were (secret 3). He took white space to look beneath the surface at the invisible essentials and used empathy to connect. He sneaked right past their defenses to engage in real, personal connection with the

Acceptance is a universal need that Fred Rogers amply understood.

vulnerable child in all of them. He wove these secrets together into a tapestry that led people to feel known and accepted.

Acceptance is a universal need that Fred Rogers amply understood. His acceptance messages were sometimes subtle, deftly tucked away in drawing scenes, fish-feeding occasions, and transitions. Other times they were as direct as his invitations to be his neighbor.

The Psychology of Acceptance

As we've noted, step one on the path toward acceptance of others is self-acceptance. People who have developed high self-compassion (self-acceptance) are characterized by the following traits—empathy, compassion, kindness, and connectedness—and they have a mindful perspective toward feelings, which is to say they are able to describe a range of feelings without judging them (secret 2). This accepting and compassionate attitude toward the self is thought to provide a protective buffer against some of the detrimental relational and psychological practices that are harnessed in the service of preserving *self-esteem*, such as judgment, isolation, and rumination.

In the past, self-esteem has been pursued and emphasized in school systems; however, some researchers have found that a number of problematic behaviors and psychological ills, including narcissism, self-centeredness, and a lack of concern for others, may be linked to an overfocus on self-evaluation.[7] Self-esteem has its purpose, but perhaps the emphasis on its importance has detracted from empathy development. Given our society's focus on self-esteem and the comparison culture of social media, it may seem difficult to make the shift away from social comparison toward compassion for yourself and others. If you are still wondering whether it would be worthwhile to shift to a compassionate state of mind, consider these benefits that are associated with making that shift:

- better regulated emotions and moods
- a buffer against depression

- greater self-fulfillment
- improved self-concept
- increased harmony in life[8]

Given these benefits, how do we develop this important trait? Self-acceptance requires taking full responsibility for our private worlds, which can sometimes feel like walking on broken glass. Self-acceptance researchers at Harvard University reveal this painful but liberating truth: "Change is possible only when one mindfully embraces both the responsibilities and the opportunities of decisions they have made."[9] Self-compassion requires taking an honest and kind look at our struggles.

It's true. When we come to understand the control we have over our decisions, we tend to have a greater sense of ownership over our lives, and our sense of responsibility is enhanced. Thus some believe it is important to participate in more self-judgment, fearing that a compassionate response may lead to getting stuck in problem behaviors. But this is not the case. When we beat ourselves up for our mistakes, the stress and pressure can trigger the need for the bad habits that soothed us in the first place—starting a vicious cycle. Psychological research shows that if we approach ourselves with compassion, it paves a pathway toward greater self-acceptance.[10]

Self-compassion also requires responding to oneself with kindness in the face of difficulties. It calls for the elusive balanced perspective—that fine line between being overwhelmed by emotions on the one hand and repressing them on the other. A balance requires a mindful and objective acknowledgment of emotions (secrets 2 and 5 build the foundation).

Another path toward self-acceptance is being mindful, which "involves a nonjudgmental regard for past, present and future aspects of the self, whether good or bad."[11] Although mindfulness allows us to notice the good in negative situations, it does require us to sit in awareness of hurt, trouble, and brokenness at times and joy, peace, and relaxation at others. This openness to both the pleasant and the painful, without exaggeration or minimization, allows us to be emotionally present and available to connect with neighbors. Mindfulness teaches us that the sweet is never quite so sweet without the bitter, and it bids us to experience a richer life excluding neither pleasure nor pain.

How can we accept others if we cannot accept ourselves? It is vital to do so, but many of us struggle with it. By way of mindfulness, then, self-acceptance may provide many benefits, including but not limited to

- facilitating mood regulation;
- playing a role in addressing problems with low positive emotion;
- addressing negative self-concept;
- helping to diminish those factors that put people at risk for both the onslaught and the continuation of the black cloud of depression; and
- potentially helping people experience more self-fulfilling states and harmony in life.[12]

Consider a person who has been diagnosed with post-traumatic stress disorder. They can experience anxiety, heightened startle response, difficulty sleeping, and other disruptive symptoms. However, helpers often remind clients with PTSD, "When you have gone through something traumatic, it is important to remember there is nothing wrong with you. There is something wrong with the event that happened to you. With PTSD, you are having a *normal* response to an *abnormal* circumstance." Thus—self-acceptance.

Another therapeutic strategy to increase self-acceptance is called *reframing*. My mother is good at reframing. People have often called her bossy, but she likes to say, "I am not bossy, I just have really good leadership skills." In therapy, the goal of *reframing* is to reconsider things in a positive light. The question "Is the glass half full or half empty?" is a classic way to begin reframing a situation.

When we use these strategies to develop greater self-acceptance, our sense of security also increases. And this, finally, allows for connection and relational security with others (secret 7; see also "A World without Mister Rogers"). The impact of attachment security can extend beyond close personal relationships to social relationships in general. This impact includes a host of benefits, such as

- a decreased tendency to feel threatened when interacting with people who are different from ourselves (politically, racially, and otherwise);
- a lower likelihood of feeling threatened by new circumstances;
- more tolerance of people who are different from us;
- a higher likelihood to behave in a more humane way overall; and

- a higher likelihood to give observable forms of help when needed.[13]

Self-acceptance, security, and other-acceptance go hand in hand.

The Need for Acceptance

Research interest in the parent-child bond in monkeys reveals much about attachment security.[14] The bond between infant monkeys and their mothers is all about feeding. At least, that is what we believed until a psychologist named Harry Harlow did a study. He noticed that baby monkeys that nursed on a bottle had greater survival rates than babies nursed by their mothers. So a fake mother—a bottle in a soft pad—was provided, and the baby monkeys formed strong attachments to the fake mothers.

In a follow-up study, Harlow created a sterile wire representation of a monkey, cold and lifeless, that housed a bottle for nursing. Nearby was another wire monkey, but this one was covered with a soft pad. Four monkeys were fed by the wire mother, and four others were fed by the soft mother. Both sets of monkeys had the wire and soft cloth "mothers" accessible. Which do you think they preferred?

This should come as no surprise: whether nourishment came from the cold, wire monkey mother or the soft-padded cloth mother, *all* the babies spent far more time cuddling and interacting with the soft mother. Meanwhile, the monkeys that were fed by the wire mother dismissed her after feeding.

Abraham Maslow, a renowned psychologist, developed a hierarchy of needs that motivate human beings—and some psychologists believe these needs strongly influence our mental health. Maslow postulated that we first must meet our physiological needs, such as food and rest. After physiological needs are met, then psychological needs, like safety, and higher-level needs can emerge. If needs for food and security are satiated, then Maslow's hierarchy suggests the next set of needs—"love needs"— will emerge.[15] As with the baby monkeys, although nursing is a necessary part of an infant's survival, once that need is met, the infant can move toward more psychological love needs. We see Maslow's hierarchy of needs come to life in the infant monkey pursuing his or her love needs.

We, too, have a need for love and belonging. Love needs are powerful. They may manifest in a longing to be a central part of a group of coworkers, a sports team, or a family. Maslow emphasized that at this point, we will jump hurdles to do whatever it takes to fulfill these needs for belonging and acceptance. Gang membership gives us a picture of this truth. The costs may be very high, but the desire to belong is equally strong. The same is true for the five-thousand-dollar-a-month country club fee.

Therefore, one of the greatest gifts we can give another is acceptance. Though it's often not an easy task! How easy is it for us to be accepting of another person's hostility toward us? What about anger? Or differences in worldview and values? It can be incredibly challenging to allow people to be themselves, especially when we watch our loved ones *be themselves* in ways that are at odds with our own thoughts and values. But what would happen if we allowed people to be themselves, holding them in our hearts with awe and acceptance (remember this is different from approval) as they become who they are? Maybe we could appreciate them with new eyes.

Influential therapist Carl Rogers once said, "People are just as wonderful as sunsets if I can let them be. . . . When I look at a sunset, as I did the other evening, I don't find myself saying, 'Soften the orange a bit on the right-hand corner. . . .' I don't try to control a sunset. I watch with awe as it unfolds."[16] Without acceptance, what seems to be authentic connection may in fact be an empty, phony relationship with the mental image of who we want a person to be rather than who they truly are.

In fact, we've learned that we typically don't accept influence from people who don't accept us. Looking for the truth in our neighbor's point of view (even if just a kernel) when distinct from our own is crucial. Our misguided attempts to "help" a person can backfire when we don't begin with acceptance.

Acceptance is so crucial to relationships that many counselors view it as fundamental to a counseling relationship. Carl Rogers has described how he came to learn this. Early on, when he sat down to meet with someone for therapy, he was interested in knowing how he could "change" that person. To him, people were like objects that had been broken and needed to visit a handyman for fixing.

We typically don't accept influence from people who don't accept us.

However, as he grew and developed in his practice, he wondered, "How can I provide a relationship which this person may use for *their* own personal growth?"[17] This is key to the seven secrets, which all help us to connect with our neighbor. As you may have noticed, the secrets are all about relationship. Carl Rogers believed that the higher the degree of acceptance and liking he showed to his clients, the more likely they would be able to use the relationship they developed with him in a therapeutic way.

Similarly, if someone uses their relationship with you in a therapeutic way, it may mean that by experiencing acceptance from you, they will be more likely to accept themselves. They can, perhaps, use the relationship as a microcosm of what happens in other relationships and as a safe space to talk about conflicts and receive a helpful response—fostering an emotionally corrective experience.[18]

This Mister Rogers, Carl Rogers, showed acceptance by respecting a person's feelings and attitudes moment by moment and allowing them to have their own feelings and thoughts. Most of all, he held a warm regard for each of his clients. He respected and liked them unconditionally. Carl Rogers viewed giving acceptance to others (including accepting their feelings, beliefs, and values) as a strategy for helping them to accept themselves and "become a person"—something he considered very valuable. He believed we are all islands that can reach each other by building bridges, but in order to become a person, we need to be allowed to have our own thoughts, values, and opinions. When we are truly accepted by another, despite our differences, we are helped in this process of becoming.[19]

Using the Acceptance Secret in Your Own Neighborhood

First, we have to ask ourselves, in the quietness of our hearts, if we are ready to hear the message of acceptance. Likewise, we have to examine whether we are ready to sit with our own unsettling responses.

Acceptance has been shown to be transformational in patients with overwhelming pain or terminal diagnoses. Our circumstances need not be dire in order for us to experience that change. Practicing radical acceptance can help us to prevent getting flooded with emotions, can keep our mood regulated, and can allow us to come up with more alternatives as we think clearly. Remember, other-acceptance is therapeutic, but no one can accept us *for* us. That is up to us alone.

In a culture that emphasizes performance and evaluation, success is prized over collaboration, being right over being empathetic, being beautiful on the outside over internal beauty, and division over common ground. Our climate of performance is not unique. Mister Rogers also grew up in a culture that prized outward appearances and performance. He was no stranger to judgment, and he was well acquainted with bullying. But he had a heart that was ready to receive the acceptance message of his grandfather.

If we value internal worth, then we can pay the acceptance message forward too. Does this resonate with you? Is there someone you want to remind how special they are? How you like them just as they are? Or how you enjoy their company? For example, here is a message from my late grandmother (Mims), that was written in one of her Christmas cards a few years ago:

Know that in my heart I am with you and enjoying your company amidst the Spirit of Christmas which always includes our Savior.

Love you, Mims

It is a healing balm to a grieving heart. The impact your words can have may extend beyond your lifetime, as did Grandpa McFeely's and Mims's words. Your gift of acceptance will give your words timeless relevance.

Consider adding *The Blessing: Giving the Gift of Unconditional Love and Acceptance* by John Trent and Gary Smalley to your reading list. As you read, identify how you can give messages like these to unlikely people, including parents who did not live out the messages you needed.

KEY TAKEAWAYS

- Acceptance has several forms, including self-acceptance and other-acceptance.
- Self-acceptance involves accepting oneself unconditionally as having inherent worth, despite the inevitable imperfections that come with being human.
- First accept yourself, then extend this acceptance to others.
- Acceptance doesn't mean approval.
- Self-acceptance differs from self-esteem.
- Acceptance is a universal need: We all need to belong.
- Self-acceptance requires taking an honest look at our struggles.
- Self-acceptance leads to security, which leads to other-acceptance.
- One of the greatest gifts we can give one another is acceptance.
- We typically don't accept influence from people who don't accept us, so acceptance is a must for parents, teachers, and others.

A CONCEPT TO CONTEMPLATE

Who you are right now is acceptable—unconditionally. We need acceptance from others, too, but we must know and accept ourselves before we can extend acceptance to others. If you are feeling discouraged about something, substitute your critical self-talk with the compassionate feedback you might give to a close friend with the same problem. What would you say to comfort that friend?

Establish Security

People Need to Know They Are Cared For

> Love is at the root of everything. All learning. All parenting. All relationships. Love or the lack of it.
>
> Fred Rogers, *Won't You Be My Neighbor?*

*P*eanut ran under the playpen and scooted his bottom against the wall, cowering and shrieking with pain. The Labrador puppy had just been accidentally stepped on by a clumsy human in a small room filled with other puppies. He was hurting and scared to death. Someone lifted the playpen, pulled him out, and tried to comfort him. But he was terrified. All he wanted was to hide.

The vet reported that Peanut did not seem to have any injuries from the accident, but he exhibited many of the symptoms of a disorder common in humans who have endured trauma—post-traumatic stress disorder. Peanut ran away when people tried to pet him, and he ran away when he saw the leash.

Eventually, Peanut was adopted by a woman named Grace. She knew he'd had some problems as a youngster—she had experienced childhood trauma herself. She could relate. It was a match made in heaven, and she was glad to bring him the comfort and gentleness that she wished someone could have brought her.

Grace faithfully worked with Peanut each day. She quickly learned that the dog loved to eat chicken and would do just about anything to earn a treat. Although he would not let strangers pet him, he would accept chicken out of their open hand. After a lot of time and a lot of chicken, Peanut would come to Grace when called, would excitedly approach her doing a little "happy dance" when she came home after work, and would even allow her to pick him up. He also learned to walk on a leash.

Why did this puppy who was frightened of humans allow someone to change his mind? Grace spoke to Peanut in a soothing voice when he was scared, rewarded him with treats, gave him words of affirmation, and petted him affectionately. Gradually, rather than running away from her as he had from all humans in the past, something strange happened. Peanut began running toward Grace, licking her, resting his head on her lap, and sitting close to her. Peanut began feeling more secure. When Grace was around, he even began to feel comfortable enough to venture off and explore the backyard or the house. Although he would never become a therapy dog, he was a dog with a therapeutic story because he was able to overcome his fears and anxieties and find a loving connection with his human.

Many of us feel like Peanut at times. We're scared of connecting, hurt from being stepped on, timid, and longing
to hide in a safe place of comfort. But with enough grace
and healing relationships, we can—with much time and
patience—move from an insecure place to a more secure place
because it is possible to rebuild trust and a sense of safety.
We can help others, just as Grace helped Peanut, by letting
them know they are safe and valued.

Express Care to Help Establish Security

As the title of this chapter hints, it is important to let people
know they are cared for. We know that when someone like
Mercy from the last chapter is threatened, stressed, hurt, sad,
or otherwise compromised, she may feel insecure. Looking
at those insecure feelings through a psychological lens, we
know this means her attachment system has been activated—
compelling her to seek out safety and security—and it is
human nature for her to first seek out a comforting attachment figure. This helps her make sense of her feelings in a
safe place and moment where she knows she is valued and
cared for regardless of performance. In the absence of any
comforting figure or safe place, further psychological distress
can occur. But as we learned, Mercy found Mister Rogers in
her moment of distress, and he knew how to use expressions
of care to help her and his other viewers feel secure.

We can learn from Mister Rogers not only that it is possible to deliver authentic expressions of care to many people
but also *how* to do so. He started with acceptance: "It's
you I like." Sometimes he added a song. Sometimes he even
personalized the song to the individual. He shared these

expressions with regularity, at expected times during the program. He emphasized the uniqueness of each person and that he liked us as we were. He also expressed that each of us was wanted—he wanted us to be *his* neighbor.

Again, he not only told us but also sang to us about this secure invitation in his song "Won't You Be My Neighbor?" It was as if he understood how fickle our memory can sometimes be—he went on to ask us that question not once but eight different times. He said please three times and repeated that he had always wanted a neighbor just like us. He left no room for doubt. This was not a question that would trigger confusion but one that cultivated certainty. Rogers understood our human need for reassurance and security.

He started and ended each episode with an expression of care—love, if you will. He knew that love is what matters most in the world. Rogers invited us into relationship and let us know how he felt about us. Psychological research suggests that people tend to remember best the first and last thing they hear and forget what is in the middle.[1] And the most memorable segments of Mister Rogers's program were clear expressions of care. He wanted us to remember above all else that we are loved and cared for as we are.

> *He started and ended each episode with an expression of care—love, if you will. He knew that love is what matters most in the world.*

Repetition is key. This made his programming not only informative but also formative because his programs allowed viewers to be experientially influenced by his authentic feelings for them. After filming an episode, François Clemmons, the African-American police officer on *Mister Rogers'*

Neighborhood, heard Mister Rogers say his usual expression of care: "You have made today a special day just by being you." And Officer Clemmons asked, "Fred, were you talking to me?" Rogers responded, "Yes. I've been talking to you for two years, but you heard me today."[2] He has been talking to all of us for years. Have you heard him yet?

Benefits of Expressing Care

Some benefits of giving and receiving an expression of care are clear—like a feeling of connection and a sense of safety and security. But there are other, perhaps less apparent, benefits as well.

Take resilience, for example, which is the ability to adjust to or recover from changes or setbacks. When people get thrown around by life, their ability to bounce back from these adverse circumstances is determined by their resilience. Girls tend to be more resilient due to the construction of their relationships that usually are warm and caring (as opposed to boys, whose relationships with other boys tend to be more competitive).[3] The three love languages that contribute most to resilience include acts of service, quality time, and words of affirmation.[4] Thus taking time to express care and affirming words to others may lead to helping them gain more bounce back in their lives. The ability to bounce back can make life much more fulfilling.

Research on attachment also shows that if children develop secure attachment bonds with a caring adult, it is likely that they will be more successful at managing bad moods and painful emotions than their peers with nonsecure styles. They will also tend to trust and have faith that their relationship partners will be there for them.[5] Not only does cultivating safe attachment relationships and sharing expressions of care lead to ease in managing emotions and trusting relationship partners, but it may also be linked with greater hope and provide a buffer against burnout.[6]

As children grow and develop over time, if they have consistent responsiveness and availability from their parents, they are likely to develop a *secure attachment style*. This means that if they skin their knee or get scared, they will turn to and move toward their attachment figure. But many of us grow up without such responsive care. If a child has not had consistent responsiveness from an attachment figure, he or she develops an insecure attachment style and has a tendency to turn away from emotional support and/or get tangled up in unpleasant feelings.

What is a child without these responsive caregivers to do? Those who recognize and turn to a kind and trustworthy adult such as Mister Rogers, a teacher, a coach, a Sunday school teacher, or a youth leader can develop a secure style just like those who were born into more secure families. What is important is that someone along the way shows them what love is. Learning to love by experiencing love from others helps to develop a more secure style of relating to others. Hearing the voice of a kind, loving, and receptive parent or mentor echoed again and again sets people up to become so familiar with the voice of those expressions of care that they internalize them and develop a kind of internal parent to reassure themselves when that person is absent.[7]

Rogers understood these benefits of expressing care— and he also understood that expressions of care are not a one-way street. The power is in both the giving and receiving of them.

Giving and receiving expressions of care were two sides of the same coin for Mister Rogers. He once confessed in an interview with Charlie Rose that his soul was not fed by the "fancy people" of the world and that he wanted to be able to gracefully receive hugs from many "neighbors," including those he met unexpectedly. "Because," he explained, "I think graceful receiving is one of the most wonderful gifts we can give anyone."[8]

The Mister Rogers Effect: Gracefully Receiving Expressions of Care

We have seen how Mister Rogers so adeptly communicated expressions of care. He also gave the gift of gracefully *receiving* care, as in this story where his soul was nourished and a boy's life was transformed.

There was a young man who was suffering a great deal, struggling to maintain the hope to live. This fourteen-year-old boy's cerebral palsy usually left him unable to speak or move freely. He used a computer to "speak" for him, but his condition left him vulnerable to the cruelty of others and did not prevent him from thinking or feeling poorly about himself. The frustration, anger, and pain became so intense that at times, he began to hit himself repeatedly. Over time, that wasn't enough to distract himself from the pain. The young man's pain must have been overwhelming, because, sadly, he began using his computer to tell his mother that he did not want to live anymore "for he was sure that God didn't like what was inside him any more than he did." Apart from the pain and suffering he experienced, there was one thing that was different—one thing that brought him joy. He loved watching *Mister Rogers' Neighborhood.*

The boy's mother, seeing him suffer, thought that perhaps Mister Rogers was keeping her son alive. They lived in California and Rogers in Pennsylvania. The thought of her son meeting Mister Rogers seemed impossible because travel would have been a severe struggle for her son. Then one day, it wasn't so impossible.

Through a foundation that was designed to help children like her son, the boy's mother found out that Mister Rogers was traveling to California. He made plans to visit her son after meeting Koko the gorilla. (Koko was also a fan; she greeted him with a hug and took off his shoes. But that is another story.)[9]

The boy's initial reaction was surprising. He did like Mister Rogers, but when he heard Rogers was there for a visit, the boy became so nervous that he was overwhelmed with self-hatred and anger and began hitting himself. His mom had to take him out of the room. Patiently, Rogers waited.

He had a request for his fourteen-year-old television neighbor. Rogers wanted the boy to pray for him. Why? Because he believed anyone who had been through such difficulty must be close to God.

This must have been shocking to the young boy, who was struggling with self-hatred. Mister Fred Rogers—singer, narrator, puppeteer, and television program host—wanted *his* prayers.

This was a totally unexpected request. Tom Junod, one of Rogers's journalist friends, wrote that when the boy heard this, he was "thunderstruck."

The boy agreed; he would try his best to pray for Mister Rogers. That day changed the boy's life; it was a new beginning. From that day on, he never spoke of wanting his life to end. He began something new. He began praying for Mister Rogers.[10]

Mister Rogers had a profound effect on the young man, whom he visited once in person and many times through "television visits." The boy now knew Mister Rogers liked him, and since Mister Rogers was close to God, the boy concluded God must like him too.

Rogers believed everything is about love, and he showed this young boy that the love he had to give was valuable. Rogers also believed the most important things we can help children understand are how to *give* and *receive love*. Through this interaction and gentle wisdom, Mister Rogers enabled this boy to love him, by requesting the young man's expressions of care through prayer. Rogers enabled this boy, who thought himself unlovely, to discover love.

The Psychology of Expressing Care

Mister Rogers closed every television show by reminding children that they were cared for. He encouraged them to go out into the world with an open attitude to learn and grow. This is an important concept: expressions of *care* cannot be understood apart from acceptance. Psychiatrist Dr. John Kuhnley often shares this message of acceptance with his patients and finds that it resonates with those who are struggling with feelings of failure or thoughts of suicide: "What I am today is good enough [acceptance], what I will be tomorrow—even better [growth]."[11] This capacity to accept oneself and seek to grow arises from a secure state of mind; thus acceptance and expressions of care are relational secrets that go hand in hand.

To make expressions of acceptance and caring impactful, of course, requires security. It's important to be genuine, consistent, and congruent. (Dr. Carl Rogers once said that authenticity was so important that if he found himself perpetually disliking his clients, it would be better to express it.[12] I literally laughed out loud when I heard this. Not only may it not seem therapeutic but it was not in his character because he cared for his clients and even prized them. However, he, like Mister Fred Rogers, valued congruence and authenticity.)

What does congruence mean? If you are strong in congruence, it means you give clear and consistent messages, and you are all together in one piece rather than fragmented or sending mixed signals. This means your thoughts and feelings are in alignment, your behaviors and goals are in alignment, and your values and behaviors are consistent. Or in Rogers's case, you are the same person on and off the screen. We can never be perfect at absolute congruence, but we can move in that direction.

Rogers combined his expressions of care with the action of helping children make sense of their feelings about good-byes. For example, he communicated that we would see each other again, and in the meantime, we could look for things we wanted to chat about, and he would too. He also spoke with genuineness, making his expressions of care believable and powerful. If we lean in, and listen attentively to what Rogers is saying, maybe, like Officer Clemmons, we will hear something new for the first time.

Activating the Attachment System

What is at work psychologically when expressions of care are put into words is the awakening of an ancient biological system. A system that connects the giver and receiver is activated. This ancient system is present in every child at birth—the *attachment system.*

We have an excellent example of this system. Some years ago, I attended a seminar by Dr. Bob Marvin. He had come to speak to my department about his work. As an undergraduate, Marvin was a student research associate for Dr. Mary Ainsworth, who had worked with Dr. John Bowlby. A noted child psychologist, Bowlby was the founder and developer of attachment theory—the theory that explains nearly everything about relationships and can allow us to predict relational style from one generation to another with over 75 percent accuracy.[13] Those are pretty good odds for inferential statistics.

Dr. Marvin spent his life working with Dr. Ainsworth and continues to run a clinic in her name even now, twenty years after her death. From Bowlby to Ainsworth to Marvin, we could trace all the life-changing work on attachment theory to that moment in our lecture hall. Dr. Marvin explained how he teaches key tenets of attachment theory to parents, using the technique he calls the Circle of Security. During our visit, my colleague Dr. Kevin Van Wynsberg asked a question that I want to pass on.

"Dr. Marvin, we train counselors. So if you could share only one thing, from your years of working with Mary Ainsworth and studying attachment that you would want counselors to know, what would it be?"

Dr. Marvin paused for a moment. His gray hair settled as he tilted his head up toward the ceiling as if in deep thought, and then he exclaimed, "I would want to show them a comic!"

He then brought up a comic strip on his computer that showed a child who looked fully depleted, head hanging, eyes averted.

The next frame showed a parent sitting on a couch, their arms outstretched, and the word *Recharger*. The frame after that showed the child in the parent's arms "recharging." The last frame showed the child squirming around, ready to break away and explore, indicated by the "full charge indicator wiggle." Here we could see the child's attachment system activated, recharged, then powered off so the exploration system could power on. After recharging, he is ready to go out and explore the world.[14]

Once the child goes off to explore, glancing back periodically just for the reassurance that his parent is still there and available, he is able to explore and engage with his environment in a productive way. This reassurance fulfills the needs of the attachment system.

There is hope even if these conditions of safety and security offered by a responsive parent aren't present. Life offers

second chances and new opportunities for other attachment figures to help us become relationally secure. Mister Rogers provided a second chance for kids like Mercy from secret 6. He reminded her that he was happy to see her and that she was special, even though other people or experiences told her otherwise.

There's a lot of wisdom in that simple comic. Children need to know there is at least *one* adult who will be available reliably and consistently to provide safety and care during times of need.

Life offers second chances and new opportunities for other attachment figures to help us become relationally secure.

As we've noted, Mister Rogers ended every program with his expressions of care, which had the effect of putting viewers' attachment systems to rest with secure base messages and preparing them to go out and explore their environments with curiosity and wonder. He let us know he cared about us and would be a reliable presence. For example, in his closing song, he reminded us that he would be back. He also always ended his programs by letting us know how he felt about us—with him we were all liked and wanted—and encouraging us to come back with things we wanted to talk about. He would thus recharge our attachment systems and leave viewers with "fully charged cells capable of anything."[15] He helped us feel safe; he let us know that he was available via television. He was a substitute attachment figure, offering a revisionist agenda for the attachment history of many children and adults alike.[16] Mister Rogers knew the three things that people from three to one hundred and three most need to transition securely.

1. People need expressions of care to help recharge their batteries. Mister Rogers's inclusion of these expressions was a rarity among children's television programs.

2. A sustained, available, safe, warm, caring attachment figure to recharge with, even via television, can make a difference. Attachment priming means taking a mental picture of an attachment figure and spending time thinking about that person.[17]

3. We have a human need to know that our attachment relationships have some permanence. Mister Rogers understood this and would remind children that he would see them again in the next program.

Attachment and Security

I'm fascinated that we can use attachment research to predict the way a baby will respond to parenting as a child and an adolescent. These trends will also likely show us how they will parent their own children.

Attachment explains so much about human behavior and why we act the way we do![18] (Remember the four attachment styles: secure, preoccupied, dismissing, and unresolved.) The idea that you are stuck with the attachment system you have has become passé. Attachment research teaches us that your past experiences don't matter as much as how you respond to and make sense of those experiences. If you respond with forgiveness and acceptance, integrating both into the story that has made you who you are today, then despite difficult experiences, you can develop a secure attachment style.[19] What is most significant in your interpersonal history is not the events but how *you* talk about them. If you can share the story of your relational history in a clear and coherent manner, then a sense of relational security can emerge regardless of the painful reality of your interpersonal history.

Letting a person know that you care, often referred to as "valuing of the person," is central to good, secure relationships. Dr. Carl Rogers called these expressions of care the demonstration of *unconditional positive regard*, which means that a person is accepted without condition.[20] They are cared for just for being themselves. Sound familiar? This is not unlike Mister Rogers's message to children. It turns out this is a healing message for people of all ages. This secret, although distinct from the secret of acceptance, goes hand in hand with acceptance. How can you care about someone if you do not accept them as they are?

> What is most significant in your interpersonal history is not the events but how *you* talk about them.

Mister Rogers accepted others and had an effect that continues to manifest. Consider some of these comments from faculty and research team students in the behavioral sciences who were asked about the effect Mister Rogers had on them:

- "He was my hero." Dr. Lisa Sosin, director of PhD in counselor education and supervision
- "What I learned from him was that I could be *all* man and still be sensitive, gentle, and kind." Dr. Kevin Hull, assistant professor of counseling

- "I think there are things [Mister Rogers did] that can speak to anyone, no matter who they are or what they have been through." Dr. Kristin Hauswirth, doctoral teaching assistant and resident in counseling

- "Growing up he was a source of comfort. Turning on the TV and watching him put on a new sweater each day made me feel welcomed." Emma Dimondi, counseling student

Using the Security Secret in Your Own Neighborhood

We've talked a lot about parents letting children know they are cared for, but as teachers, coaches, and bosses, and even as friends and coworkers, we can bring the message of acceptance and caring to the people with whom we associate. It starts with a commitment to authenticity in our lives and empathy in our relationships. It can continue with a smile for our neighbors, eye contact and a nod toward a passerby, and perhaps taking a moment to truly listen and demonstrate care when we ask our neighbor how they are doing. There are many ways we can practice care by seeking to see the best in our neighbors and ourselves.

This sets a good example for others. We can help children learn that they, too, can care for others, even starting with things like caring for plants, fish, or other pets.

Clients who are struggling with depression and thoughts of suicide have shared with me that small gestures, such as a smile from a stranger, have reminded them that there is goodness in the world and helped them find the will to continue living. You never know the power of your expressions of care. Even small gestures can make a difference.

It bears repeating that authenticity is key. When are you your most authentic self? What practices or situations give you the courage to be yourself? Faith was important to Mister Rogers. He spent time each morning engaged in his faith practice, which involved praying for a long list of people by name. This was one way he expressed care. If you practice a particular faith tradition, how can you express soul care for your loved ones? I believe if Mister Rogers were part of this discussion, he would invite us to do something he did in every speech he gave. He would invite us to take a moment of silence to think of all the people who have loved us into becoming who we are. Here's how. Set a timer on your phone for one minute and, in honor of Mister Rogers, take that time to think about people in your life who have loved you into becoming. Remember, as he reminded us, they may be someone close by or they may be someone who lives far away. Maybe the person you think of is in heaven.

A simple strategy for emulating Rogers's effusive expressions of care is to develop an expression of care in writing and share it with a loved one. Here's a way to approach it. With pen and paper in hand (and perhaps a cup of tea), write your responses to the following questions:

- Who did you think of during this time?
- How did they encourage you?
- How did their expressions of care shape who you have become?
- Whose list do you want to be on?
- How would you want them to answer these questions?

Write out an expression of care that you can share with a loved one. If you have trouble identifying a person you would like to share this message with, you may alternatively think of someone you would like to influence. Like bodies of water change the lands they run through over time, we are shaped and impacted by those who love us. If we do not know someone cares, it is challenging to accept their influence. So those you express care for regularly will also likely be those that you influence.

Mims, my grandmother, often comes to mind when I do this exercise. When I was a young adult, I experienced a lot of trauma. After helping me develop a safety plan, Mims encouraged me to forgive the person who had caused the trauma, bless them, and leave the rest in God's hands. She wrote me reminders on how to do this. Her advice and encouragement gave me the emotional strength to keep my heart soft, rather than hardening it to cope with the pain.

Like bodies of water change the lands they run through over time, we are shaped and impacted by those who love us.

Mims taught me a strength of character that allowed me to lean into a difficult situation and look at it as an opportunity to bless someone I was not inclined to bless and to thereby release any power they had to harm me. I owe her a debt of gratitude and love I can never repay.

I also think of Mister Rogers, for many of the reasons we have discussed throughout this book. If it was hard to think of someone that loved you into becoming, consider watching the documentary about Mister Rogers, *Won't You Be My Neighbor?* Allow his work and his kindness to love you into becoming more of who you really are through reading his books and watching episodes of his program.

KEY TAKEAWAYS

- Establishing a sense of security in our children is one of the most important things parents and other caregivers can do.
- It is human nature to seek out a comforting attachment figure to help us make sense of our feelings.
- Letting people know they are cared for gives them a sense of security through which they can navigate life.
- Caring for ourselves and others is one of the most important things we can teach.
- Along with expressing care to others, we need to gracefully receive care from others.
- It is possible to deliver authentic expressions of care, starting with self-acceptance and then moving on to other-acceptance. Seek to tell others they are loved and cared for as they are.
- Repetition is key.
- Expressions of care go hand in hand with acceptance. We have to accept someone before we can authentically care for someone.
- People who receive messages of care are more resilient.
- People who have developed secure attachments/ relationships will be more successful at managing negative emotions.

- The capacity to accept oneself and seek to grow arises from a secure state of mind.

- To make expressions of acceptance and caring effective, you must be believable, authentic, genuine, consistent—in other words, congruent.

- Congruence means having consistency. This can be consistency in your feelings and words, thoughts and actions, and internal and external communication.

- Attachment theory, and the principles by which it operates, explains a lot about human behavior and should be considered a way to understand relational dynamics.

A CONCEPT TO CONTEMPLATE

People need to know they are cared for. Acceptance, authenticity, and consistency help establish security in our relationships with others. Contemplate how you feel and behave when you sense you are secure (supported, cared for, loved, and safe). How would life be different if you always felt secure? How would your actions differ?

Closing Thoughts

Does Mister Rogers Still Live
in Your Neighborhood?

As human beings, our job in life is to help people realize
how rare and valuable each one of us really is, that each
of us has something that no one else has—or ever will
have—something inside that is unique to all time. It's
our job to encourage each other to discover that uniqueness and to provide ways of developing its expression.

Fred Rogers, *The World According to Mister Rogers*

*L*et's take some time to look back on what has been
discussed and how the pieces of the puzzle fit together. The seven secrets (psychological principles) in this
text are synergistic, and Mister Rogers often used them in
concert with one another.

Rogers was keen on making it clear that there is no shame
in expressing feelings. Without someone to remind us of that,

both individually and as a society, it is easy to let what author Brené Brown calls the "shame gremlins" take over.[1] Shame gremlins tell us it is not okay to feel and it is certainly not okay to express vulnerable feelings such as sadness, missing, valuing, or anything that rebuffs myths of rugged individualism or suggests we crave community. Mister Rogers believed that if we all could learn how to express our feelings through appropriate outlets, the world would be a safer place for tomorrow's children. We all need to be reminded of this universal truth: helping people manage emotions today creates a safer tomorrow for our children and our neighbors. We need the Mister Rogers effect now more than ever.

During his lifetime, Mister Rogers had quite an effect on this world. He produced over eight hundred television shows, acting as the puppeteer and cowriter for all the songs and scripts for each episode. Of course, he was always quick to credit his musical director, Johnny Costa, and all the others who helped make the show possible. He also received two Peabody Awards, a Presidential Medal of Freedom, and over forty honorary degrees. He was the author of many books and hundreds of letters that made a difference in the lives of fans and those they shared the letters with. Let's take one last look at the seven key principles that were woven throughout Mister Rogers's work.

Secret 1: Listen First

We started with the importance of taking the time to listen to our neighbors. Although Rogers could not listen to all of his television neighbors individually, he did listen to his mentor, Dr. Margaret McFarland, which enabled him to give people of all ages the sense that they were heard and understood. Someone who listens well allows us to feel seen for who we are on the inside because true knowing lends itself to true loving. It takes extra effort to truly listen to understand, but it leads to powerful intellectual connections that eradicate loneliness. If you could take only one thing from this secret, remember that listening is the first step to loving. As we hear a person's heart, we get to know that person better, which allows us to get closer to truly loving that person. Remember to use active listening (paraphrase back what you are hearing in an empathetic tone) to help your loved ones and neighbors feel heard.

Secret 2: Validate Feelings

From there, we explored the key theme of validating feelings. Ironically, sometimes parents hold back on validating feelings for fear of encouraging them or making them more intense. On the contrary, validating a feeling often has an opposite effect. Once we have been heard and understood, we can begin to let go of the intensity of an emotion. Although it can be uncomfortable to talk with people about their difficult emotions, doing so fosters a powerful emotional connection that enables a person to feel emotionally held without ever being touched. Be willing to be present with other people's emotions, take the time to ask how they are feeling—and be courageous enough to listen to the answers.

One of the most important things we can learn from Mister Rogers about feelings is that it is important to create a safe place for both ourselves and others to talk about sometimes difficult topics (e.g., divorce, death, jealousy, forgiveness) and the feelings that go with them. When we talk about our feelings, they do not seem as overwhelming, and we can also talk about ways to manage them. For example, when we feel angry, we can stop before we do something that could be harmful to ourselves or others and do something else instead.

Notice this secret requires listening to our own hearts and those of others, thus secrets 1 and 2 go hand in hand.

Secret 3: Pause and Think

In an interview Rogers lamented that we live in such a noisy world, and he wondered, "How do we encourage reflection?" Mister Rogers invited us to make more room for wonder because it allows us to take an interest in others and our environment with a desire to seek to understand and experience joy. Wonder helps us to be present in the moment and see the world and our neighbors with new eyes. In a world anesthetized by the constant barrage of information, he was awake to the importance of stillness and wonder.

> *Mister Rogers invited us to make more room for wonder because it allows us to take an interest in others and our environment.*

Rogers charged us—his like-minded neighbors—to find ways to make time for silence and white space. It is important to start with ourselves, hollowing out white space on our calendars to be with our own thoughts. Maybe this means taking a long drive, or some time journaling, or a cup of tea while gazing out at the deep blue sea. Extending this to our neighbors could mean inviting them to reflect with us on a good movie or interrupting the volleying of conversation with thoughtful, pregnant pauses—silence that allows ideas to be birthed. Inviting others to pause with us to take in a sunset or admire the short-lived blossom of the cherry blossom tree may only take a few moments, but small steps can add up to high mileage.

Mister Rogers wanted us to remember to look for the invisible in our neighbor—the internal characteristic or feature that's woven into the fabric of their soul that makes them unique and special. Looking with this new perspective allows us to see past the roughest exterior to a diamond in the rough. He saw himself as an emotional archeologist, who was always looking for the roots of things. We can look beneath the surface too.[2]

Secret 4: Show Gratitude

Rogers often used phrases that distributed the spirit of gratitude. Gratitude, as it turns out, is incredibly good for our health and relationships. Research unveils gratitude's role in optimizing our brains, our moods, our health, and our relationships. Embracing the principle of gratitude is life changing. Just in the writing of this book, I have sent out more thank-you cards than perhaps ever before, and I've enjoyed the process immensely.

> *Gratitude is incredibly good for our health and relationships.*

When Mister Rogers spoke, he always left people some white space for reflection (secrets 3 and 4 go together like socks and shoes). He specifically asked them to reflect on whom they were grateful for, who had been the difference makers who had "loved them into becoming."

Secret 5: Develop Empathy

We often hear empathy described with the classic metaphor of walking a mile in another person's shoes, but there's more to it than that. True empathy feels what another person feels from *their* frame of reference—actually understanding their story and feeling, in part, what they feel about it. In other words, empathy involves seeking to experience the world as others do. It also requires the courage to be vulnerable and connect to a similar feeling in ourselves.

Empathy plays an important role in human happiness. Roots of empathy may be found in the earliest of interpersonal encounters: a baby smiles and his mother smiles back at him and the baby smiles again. Empathy promotes relationships. If you fail to learn empathy, relationships with others are filled with less love, and without love, frankly, it's difficult to experience authentic connection and authentic happiness.

Mister Rogers also believed we have to love ourselves before we can truly love others. Meaning that empathy requires being open to our own feelings. If we close the door to our feelings, we not only stuff away the unpleasant but we miss being present to the good. Remember, Mister Rogers would tell you that he likes you just the way you are (and that includes your feelings).

Secret 6: Practice Acceptance

Acceptance was a key principle that helped Mister Rogers empathize and validate others' feelings. The value of acceptance extends to others, but self-acceptance is a *prerequisite* for other-acceptance. We must start there. Self-acceptance involves accepting oneself unconditionally as having inherent worth, despite the inevitable imperfections that come with being human.

Acceptance is a universal need; we all need to belong. Once we've learned to accept ourselves as we are, we can begin to extend that same unconditional acceptance to others. We don't have to approve—just accept.

> *Self-acceptance is a prerequisite for other-acceptance. We must start there.*

Acceptance is crucial to all human relationships, whether family relationships, friendships, or relationships with teachers, mentors, or others.

Secret 7: Establish Security

Communicating our expressions of care to others is important, because it helps to establish a sense of security within them. Knowing you are cared for helps you to feel secure within yourself and with your place in the world. People who feel secure are also resilient—they can deal with setbacks and manage their emotions well.

Authenticity is important in expressing care, and consistency and repetition are key. We all need to be reminded that we are loved and cared for. Also security requires acceptance, and expressions of care cannot be understood apart from acceptance.

Each secret (key principle) explored throughout this book worked together to allow Mister Rogers to provide a haven of safety for his viewers.

Let's Take a Moment

Remember, Mister Rogers had a habit that transformed his audiences. Each time he had an opportunity to address a crowd (whether at a college graduation, an award ceremony, or another public event), he would take time to express gratitude for all those who had "loved him into becoming," and he would honor them with a moment of silence. This became one of his habits. Notice how he used both gratitude and white space. He would then encourage his audience to do the same—implementing both empathy and gratitude. He reminded them that this could include people who were nearby, far away, or even in heaven. Then he'd give his audience some time to think of those folks as he offered to keep time. Let's do the same. Would you, in honor of Mister Rogers and all those who have loved you into becoming, take a minute to think of those special ones? Let's take just a minute to think of them.

This practice helps us to develop empathy for those loved ones. As I mentioned before, I think of my Mims, who is in heaven. She loved me into becoming in many ways. For example, I finished my undergraduate degree in business but somehow I knew I was not cut out for sales. I was the kind of person who needed to feel like I was helping people in ways that seemed more meaningful or tangible to me. Mims knew this about me too. She encouraged me to go to a university preview weekend. And when I did, I heard about a counseling program, which started me on the trajectory of my career. Of course, that made a huge difference in my life. If it were not for Mims, I would not be teaching and counseling, and this book would not be here. Even before that, she believed in me when I was going through some dark times as a teenager. The kindness, love, and care she showed me during that season made the difference of a lifetime. She believed in me—even when I did not believe in myself.

Sometimes it is hard to articulate how someone has made a difference because they have impacted us in so many ways, but taking the time to thank them helps us use the key principles of white space/reflection, gratitude, and (if we go on to express it to them) expressions of care.

Maybe you thought of a parent or relative during our white space moment. But perhaps when a neighbor, friend, child, student, or client of yours picks up this book, they will stop and think of *you*. Maybe you will be one of those very special people who loved them into becoming. Maybe your expressions of care and kindness have changed a life.

Did you identify whose list you would like to be on? Who are the people in your "neighborhood" that you feel compelled to love into becoming? Maybe it is a coworker, a mentee, a child, a neighbor, a friend, a cousin, a student, or a barista at the local coffee shop. The greatest outcome of this book would be you answering that question and seeking to make a difference for them by sharing Mister Rogers's lessons. Sometimes we even have a chance to do this for someone who may never know our name.

A Reminder for the Journey

"All of us, at some time or other, need help. Whether we're giving or receiving help, each one of us has something valuable to bring to this world. That's one of the things that connects us as neighbors—in our own way, each one of us is a giver and a receiver."[3]

Mister Rogers did not leave us without the comfort he brought. He left us with one another. Remember that the care he has shown you is something you will always have "in the way down deep inside you." Let's remember it and share what he taught us with our neighbors.

Now imagine both Mister Rogers and me telling you this together. Please store it in your heart and share it with your neighbors so we can work together to make it seem like Mister Rogers still lives in our neighborhood.

Neighbor, you have made today a special day just by your being you. There is no one else in the whole world like you, and I like you just the way you are.

Acknowledgments

*T*o my Mims, Ida Molina-Zinam, who always brought out the best in me, who was a great encourager and believer in the project. Thanks.

Overwhelming gratitude to Jamie Chavez, who invested countless hours editing and revising this book, transforming a large manuscript into a much more condensed version. This book would not have reached its potential without her skillful edits. I will forever owe a debt of gratitude to Jamie. She artfully brought out the best in this manuscript and has helped increase the likelihood that this text may be worthy of its subject matter. Jamie's humor, empathy, and adeptness all blessed me during this process.

To Rachel Jacobson, who brought out the best in me and my work. Rachel believed in the power of this manuscript and championed it. She worked to tighten it and provided important edits and helpful counsel that have been of great value throughout this process.

Much appreciation goes to Robin Turici for her careful edits and fine-tuning of the final manuscript, endnotes, and other details to ensure the utmost accuracy and attention to detail. Thank you for your efforts that brought this work through the final stages.

I would like to thank Jim Hart, who understood the value of Rogers's work and believed in the importance of sharing this manuscript. Jim took great care to make sure it was in the good hands of those who believed in the vision of this text.

To Emily Grace Culver, whose input and knowledge of Chicago style have been invaluable and much appreciated. And to Tram Nguyen and Rachel Birkeland, whose tireless research assistance, time spent scouring the literature, and thoughtful help verifying the accuracy and organization of the endnotes is much appreciated.

Special thanks to Charles Mike Molina for his careful hours spent reviewing and making helpful suggestions for enhancing this manuscript. His long hours and careful input have contributed to the quality of this book.

My deepest gratitude to Mister Fred Rogers for devoting his life to making a difference through his work, his kindness, and his expressions of care. I also appreciate his mentor, Dr. Margaret McFarland, who helped him learn so many therapeutic concepts and helped him to develop as America's television therapist. Thanks to the Fred Rogers Center at Saint Vincent College for the 143 Club, for the opportunity to be a part of Rogers's legacy, and for continuing to share the work for all of us to benefit from. I am thankful that you have shared the legacy of Fred Rogers with generations to come.

Special thanks to Joanne Rogers for her heartfelt writings in the forewords of several books that captured the spirit of her husband's life and work and inspired me and many others.

Thanks to all of Mister Rogers's journalist friends who shared their stories and encounters with his healing personality.

Deepest gratitude to WQED and all those who continue to keep Mister Rogers's work alive by making it available online, in movies, and on DVDs or otherwise.

Thank you to the panel of experts and researchers who performed the qualitative analysis and other research or commentary that informed this book: Dr. E. John Kuhnley, Dr. R. Justin Silvey, Kristin Hauswirth, Tram Nguyen, Rachel Birkeland, Dr. Robyn Simmons, Dr. Kevin Hull, Dr. Lisa Sosin, Dorin Captari-Scirri, Emma Dimondi, and many more.

Thank you to Kathy and Beth Usher for sharing their story of a transformative love-filled encounter with Mister Rogers.

Special thanks to all those who granted permission for their stories to be shared in this manuscript, some of whom remain nameless to protect both the guilty and the innocent.

Thanks to all who project their remembrance of Mister Rogers's countenance and kind smile onto the silhouette of his face on the cover of this text—informed by their childhood memories of him. I appreciate those who continue to keep him alive in their memories and who will help to share his character traits and everything he taught us via this book.

Heartfelt thanks to my husband, John Kuhnley, for his encouragement, enthusiasm, and love. Without you, this book would not have been possible. You are an inspiration who brings out the best in yourself and others. Thanks to my mother, who taught me to read and helped instill a love for books in me.

Thanks to my cousins—Dan Molina, Maria Molina, and Roly Molina—for sending prayers, blessings, input, and encouragement along the way. Thank you to those who prayed for and provided encouragement during the development of this project and those who were Pomodoro partners: Kristin MacDowall, Dr. Lisa Sosin, Dr. Justin Silvey, Dr. Robyn

Simmons, Nina Moser, Paul Castellanos, Ana Castellanos, Dr. Laurel Shaler, and Dr. Patti Hinkley.

Thanks to my colleagues Drs. Elias and Denise Moitinho, whose work and support have been an inspiration.

Thanks to Randy Miller, the graduate research and instruction librarian at the Jerry Falwell Library, for his skill, time, and assistance navigating databases and archives to locate original sources that informed the content in this book.

Special thanks to Gabe Robbins, who provided access to many resources, his library, and valuable lessons along the way.

To all those who have generously and thoughtfully written about or otherwise shared their encounters and experiences with Mister Rogers that have inspired this work, and to those who authored content that inspired my work, you are much appreciated: Joanne Rogers, Barry Head, Amy Hollingsworth, Tim Madigan, Tom Junod, Jeanne Marie Laskas, Charlie Rose, Antoine de Saint-Exupéry, Henry Nouwen, Dr. Carl Rogers, and many more.

Thanks to my colleagues and supervisors: Brandi Chamberlain, Kevin Van Wynesberg, and Kenyon Knapp. Your support has blessed me tremendously through this process.

Additionally, thanks to Dean Hathaway for supporting and valuing this project and for asking the hard questions. Thanks to Dr. Jacqueline Smith for your inspiring leadership and support of my writing.

Most of all, I thank my heavenly Father, who led me to discover and be blessed by the work of Fred Rogers, and to share the lessons learned along the way. I am thankful for the glimpses of His love that I saw shining through Mister Rogers's life. He, like Rogers, always sees the best in us. Both the glory and my heart rest with Him.

Notes

A World without Mister Rogers

1. "Mister Rogers on Tonight Show (1983)," YouTube video, 6:17–7:22, from interview with Joan Rivers in July 1983, posted by fwbh, May 24, 2012, https://www.youtube.com/watch?v=p-Kp5YeqrlE&feature=emb_rel_pause.

2. "Mr. Rogers – It's You I Like," YouTube video, 4:19, from *Mister Rogers' Neighborhood*, season 11, episode 4, directed by Fred Rogers, aired February 18, 1981, posted by Austin Casey, January 31, 2013, https://www.youtube.com/watch?v=5BZlyxS37Kk.

3. Amy Hollingsworth, *The Simple Faith of Mister Rogers: Spiritual Insights from the World's Most Beloved Neighbor* (Nashville: Thomas Nelson, 2005), loc. xxii, Kindle.

4. "Remembering Mr. Rogers (1994/1997) | Charlie Rose," YouTube video, 15:18, from interviews conducted in 1994 and 1997, posted by Charlie Rose, February 27, 2016, https://www.youtube.com/watch?v=djoyd46TVVc.

5. Sally Ann Flecker, "When Fred Met Margaret: Mister Rogers Mentor," PITT MED, winter 2014, https://www.pittmed.health.pitt.edu/story/when-fred-met-margaret.

6. Joanne Rogers, foreword to *Many Ways to Say I Love You: Wisdom for Parents and Children from Mister Rogers*, by Fred Rogers (New York: Hachette, 2006), 4.

7. Joanne Rogers, foreword to *Many Ways to Say I Love You*, loc. 75, Kindle.

8. "Margaret B. McFarland; Child Psychologist," *Los Angeles Times*, September 14, 1988, https://www.latimes.com/archives/la-xpm-1988-09-14-mn-1676-story.html.

9. Tim Clinton and Gary Sibcy, *Attachments: Why You Love, Feel, and Act the Way You Do* (Nashville: Thomas Nelson, 2002), 95.

10. James P. McCullough Jr. et al., "The Significant Other History: An Interpersonal-Emotional History Procedure Used with the Early-Onset Chronically Depressed Patient," *American Journal of Psychotherapy* 65, no. 3 (July 2011): 225–48, https://psychotherapy.psychiatryonline.org/doi /full/10.1176/appi.psychotherapy.2011.65.3.225.

11. For a more comprehensive discussion, see *Attached: The New Science of Adult Attachment and How It Can Help You Find and Keep Love* by Amir Levine and Rachel Heller; *Redeeming Attachment: A Counselor's Guide to Facilitating Attachment to God and Earned Security* by Anita M. Knight and Gary Sibcy; or *Attachments: Why You Love, Feel and Act the Way You Do* by Tim Clinton and Gary Sibcy.

12. "Remembering Mr. Rogers (1994/1997) | Charlie Rose," YouTube video.

13. Rainer Maria Rilke, *Letters to a Young Poet*, trans. Stephen Mitchell (New York: Random House, 1984), 34–35.

The Mister Rogers Effect

1. "Won't You Be My Neighbor? (2018)—Mister Rogers & Jeff Erlanger Scene (8/10) | Movieclips," YouTube video, 3:23, from *Mister Rogers' Neighborhood*, season 11, episode 4, directed by Fred Rogers, aired February 18, 1981, posted by Movieclips, January 10, 2019, https://www .youtube.com/watch?v=USWXF1XW2zo; and "Mr. Rogers—It's You I Like," YouTube video, 6:50.

2. "Fred Rogers Inducted into the TV Hall of Fame," YouTube video, 5:59, from Television Hall of Fame induction in 1999, posted by Julian Park, April 9, 2012, https://www.youtube.com/watch?v=TcNxY4TudXo &app=desktop.

3. Rob Owen, "Obituary: Jeff Erlanger / Quadriplegic Who Endeared Himself to Mister Rogers," *Pittsburgh Post-Gazette*, June 14, 2007, https:// www.post-gazette.com/news/obituaries/2007/06/14/Obituary-Jeffrey-Erlan ger-Quadriplegic-who-endeared-himself-to-Mister-Rogers/stories/2007061 40325; and Daniel Lewis, "Mister Rogers, TV's Friend for Children, Is Dead at 74," *New York Times*, February 28, 2003, https://www.nytimes.com /2003/02/28/arts/mister-rogers-tv-s-friend-for-children-is-dead-at-74.html.

4. Jennifer V, comment on "Mister Rogers on The Rosie O'Donnell Show," YouTube video, 6:46, from interview on *The Rosie O'Donnell Show* in 1996, posted by fwbh, July 1, 2009, https://www.youtube.com /watch?v=5_84_5_c1GE.

5. qqq, comment on "Mister Rogers on The Rosie O'Donnell Show."

6. Comment on "Mister Rogers on The Rosie O'Donnell Show."

7. Amin Smith, comment on "Mister Rogers on The Rosie O'Donnell Show."

8. Nietzsche's Ghost, comment on "Mister Rogers on The Rosie O'Donnell Show."

9. illuminatioracle, comment on "Mister Rogers on The Rosie O'Donnell Show."

10. bradster67, comment on "Mister Rogers on The Rosie O'Donnell Show."

11. DakariKingMykan, comment on "Mister Rogers on The Rosie O'Donnell Show."

12. Fred Rogers, *Dear Mister Rogers: Does It Ever Rain in Your Neighborhood?* (New York: Penguin Books, 1996), 127.

13. The panel I consulted included school counselor and PhD in counselor education Justin Silvey, psychiatrist Dr. Edward John Kuhnley, and clinical mental health counselor and doctoral candidate Kristin Hauswirth.

Secret 1 Listen First

1. Brenda Zalter, "The Training Miracle Question," in *Doing Something Different: Solution-Focused Brief Therapy*, ed. Thorana S. Nelson (New York: Taylor and Francis, 2010), 149.

2. David Augsburger, *Caring Enough to Hear and Be Heard: How to Hear and Be Heard in Equal Communication* (Grand Rapids: Baker, 1982), 12.

3. Mandy Len Catron, "To Fall in Love with Anyone, Do This," *New York Times*, January 9, 2015, https://www.nytimes.com/2015/01/11/style/modern-love-to-fall-in-love-with-anyone-do-this.html; and Arthur Aron et al., "The Experimental Generation of Interpersonal Closeness: A Procedure and Some Preliminary Findings," *Personality and Social Psychology Bulletin* 23, no. 4 (1997): 363–77, https://doi.org/10.1177/0146167297234003.

4. Elizabeth Usher, "When Mister Rogers Visited Me in the Hospital When I Was in a Coma," *The Mighty*, July 31, 2017, https://themighty.com/2017/07/mister-rogers-beth-usher-visited-in-hospital-brain-surgery/?fbclid=IwAR0yVQYErie4ihszIpUY7saWIj-7O98G7816LX2Bw-RAYnwt3u1qSVgHHWY.

5. Kandi L. Walker, "Do You Ever Listen? Discovering the Theoretical Underpinnings of Empathic Listening," *International Journal of Listening* 11, no. 1 (1997): 128.

6. Michael P. Nichols, *The Lost Art of Listening: How Learning to Listen Can Improve Relationships* (New York: Guilford Press, 2009), 11.

7. Nichols, *Lost Art of Listening*, 11.

8. Nichols, *Lost Art of Listening*, 11, 119.

9. Carl Weaver, *Human Listening: Process and Behavior* (Indianapolis: Bobbs-Menill, 1972), 82.

10. Nichols, *Lost Art of Listening*, 11.

11. Ronald E. Hawkins et al., *Research-Based Counseling Skills: The Art and Science of Therapeutic Empathy* (Dubuque, IA: Kendall Hunt, 2019).

12. Michael J. Lambert and Dean E. Barley, "Research Summary on the Therapeutic Relationship and Psychotherapy Outcome," *Psychotherapy: Theory, Research, Practice, Training* 38, no. 4 (2001): 358, https://psycnet .apa.org/doiLanding?doi=10.1037%2F0033-3204.38.4.357.

13. Lambert and Barley, "Research Summary," 1.

14. Walker, "Do You Ever Listen?," 128.

15. Laura E. Levine and Joyce Munsch, *Child Development: An Active Learning Approach* (Thousand Oaks, CA: Sage, 2010), 493.

16. Levine and Munsch, *Child Development*, 504.

17. Levine and Munsch, *Child Development*, 505.

18. Maxwell King, "Mr. Rogers Had a Simple Set of Rules for Talking to Children," *Atlantic*, June 8, 2018, https://www.theatlantic.com /family/archive/2018/06/mr-rogers-neighborhood-talking-to-kids/562352/.

19. Maxwell, King, *The Good Neighbor: The Life and Work of Fred Rogers* (New York: Abrams, 2018), 184; and "1502: Creativity," *Mister Rogers' Neighborhood*, directed by Paul Lally, written by Fred Rogers, 1982.

20. King, "Mr. Rogers Had a Simple Set of Rules."

21. Fred Rogers, *The World According to Mister Rogers: Important Things to Remember* (New York: Hyperion, 2003), 92.

22. Hawkins et al., *Research-Based Counseling Skills*, 75–76.

23. Hawkins et al., *Research-Based Counseling Skills*, 65.

24. Jack Zenger and Joseph Folkman, "What Great Listeners Actually Do," *Harvard Business Review*, July 4, 2016, https://hbr.org/2016/07 /what-great-listeners-actually-do.

25. Hawkins et al., *Research-Based Counseling Skills*, 46.

Secret 2 Validate Feelings

1. "Mister Rogers' Neighborhood | I'm Proud of You | PBS KIDS," YouTube video, 1:39, posted by PBS KIDS, March 20, 2017, https://www .youtube.com/watch?v=OtaK2rz-UJM.

2. "Not Seen in 35 Yrs: Mister Rogers Talks about Violence 'Not for Children Who Watch Alone,'" YouTube video, 2:19, from *Mister Rogers' Neighborhood*, posted by Kenneth Udut, October 5, 2017, https://www .youtube.com/watch?v=PDGzISvI0c8.

3. "Fred Rogers - Archive Interview Part 7 of 9 TVLEGENDS," You-Tube video, 2:03, from interview with Karen Herman, posted by tvoralhistory, February 20, 2008, https://www.youtube.com/watch?v=-GdBx 8nahMg&list=PLEFFC5735C15EE8BD.

4. "Suicide," National Institute of Mental Health, last updated April 2019, https://www.nimh.nih.gov/health/statistics/suicide.shtml.

5. James P. McCullough Jr. et al., "A Method for Conducting Intensive Psychological Studies with Early-Onset Chronically Depressed Patients," *American Journal of Psychotherapy* 64, no. 4 (2010): 317–37.

6. Moïra Mikolajczak, Clémentine Menil, and Olivier Luminet, "Explaining the Protective Effect of Trait Emotional Intelligence Regarding Occupational Stress: Exploration of Emotional Labour Processes," *Journal of Research in Personality* 41, no. 5 (2017): 1107–17, https://www.res earchgate.net/publication/222423795_Explaining_the_Protective_Effect _of_Trait_Emotional_Intelligence_Regarding_Occupational_Stress.

7. L. Van Kan, "Emotional Intelligence and Emotional Regulation: How Can We Better Manage Occupational Stress?" (master's thesis, Free University of Brussels, 2004), in Mikolajczak, Menil, and Luminet, "Explaining the Protective Effect of Trait Emotional Intelligence," 1108.

8. Marc A. Brackett and Peter Salovey, "Measuring Emotional Intelligence with the Mayer Salovery-Caruso Emotional Intelligence Test (MSCEIT)," in *Measurement of Emotional Intelligence*, ed. Glenn Geher (Hauppauge, NY: Nova Science, 2004), 179–94.

9. Oliver P. John and James J. Gross, "Healthy and Unhealthy Emotion Regulation: Personality Processes, Individual Differences, and Life Span Development," *Journal of Personality* 72 (2004): 1301–34.

10. John Harrichand, Anita Knight, and Dorin Captari, "Impact of Emotional Intelligence on Counselor Burnout," *Virginia Counselors Journal* 35 (2017): 40–47.

11. "May 1, 1969: Fred Rogers Testifies before the Senate Subcommittee on Communications," YouTube video, 6:50, posted by danieldeibler, February 8, 2015, https://www.youtube.com/watch?v=fKy7ljRr0AA.

12. James McCullough et al., "The Significant Other History: An Interpersonal-Emotional History Procedure Used with the Early-Onset Chronically Depressed Patient," *American Journal of Psychotherapy* 65, no. 3 (2018), https://doi.org/10.1176/appi.psychotherapy.2011.65.3.225.

13. Harrichand, Knight, and Captari, "Impact of Emotional Intelligence," 40–47.

14. K. V. Petrides, "Trait Emotional Intelligence Theory," *Journal of Industrial and Organizational Psychology* 3 (2010): 136–39, doi:10.1111 /j.1754–9434.2010.01213.x.

15. Harrichand, Knight, and Captari, "Impact of Emotional Intelligence," 45.

16. Maria Dolores Velarde, Gary Fry, and Mary Sundli Tveit, "Health Effects of Viewing Landscapes—Landscape Types in Environmental Psychology," *Urban Forestry & Urban Greening* 6, no. 4 (2017): 199–212, https://

www.researchgate.net/publication/223358151_Health_Effects_of_Viewing _Landscapes_-_Landscape_Types_in_Environmental_Psychology.

17. Joanne Rogers, foreword, in Fred Rogers, *Life's Journeys According to Mister Rogers: Things to Remember Along the Way* (New York: Hyperion, 2005), 9.

18. Amy Hollingsworth, *The Simple Faith of Mister Rogers: Spiritual Insights from the World's Most Beloved Neighbor* (Brentwood, TN: Integrity Publishers, 2005), 119.

19. Brian J. Taber et al., "Career Style Interview: A Contextualized Approach to Career Counseling," *Career Development Quarterly* 59, no. 3 (March 2011), 276, https://doi.org/10.1002/j.2161-0045.2011.tb00069.x.

20. "Katerina Gets Mad," Neighborhood Archive, from episode 104 of *Daniel Tiger's Neighborhood*, aired September 5, 2012, accessed April 1, 2020, http://www.neighborhoodarchive.com/dtn/episodes/104b_katerina _gets_mad/index.html.

21. Marsha Linehan, *DBT Skills Training Manual*, 2nd ed. (New York: Guilford Press, 2015), 432.

22. Linehan, *DBT Skills Training Manual*, 432.

23. Erik Hesse, "The Adult Attachment Interview: Historical and Current Perspectives," in *Handbook of Attachment: Theory, Research, and Clinical Applications*, ed. Jude Cassidy and Phillip R. Shaver (New York: Guilford Press, 1999), 395–433.

Secret 3 Pause and Think

1. *The Little Prince*, which was written by Antoine de Saint-Exupéry, has become a classic of world literature. Saint-Exupéry tells the story of a young prince who, while exploring the unknown territory of various planets, finally arrives on earth and encounters a fox. The conversational fox happens to be exceptionally wise. The fox talks with the little prince and asks the prince to tame him. The boy is confused and wants to know what this means. The fox has a habit of changing the topic but finally explains that taming, though it is one of many topics often neglected, means creating ties. The fox persuades the prince by telling him that if he tames him, the boy will be as if he is the only boy in all the world to the fox. Likewise, to the boy, the fox will then be the only fox in all the world. As they work through this process, they develop a relationship, and the boy later is ready to continue his journey. As he and the fox prepare to say their goodbyes, the fox teaches the prince a very important secret, the fourth key principle.

2. "'The Little Prince' Becomes World's Most Translated Book, Excluding Religious Works," *CTV News*, April 7, 2017, https://www.ctvnews

.ca/entertainment/the-little-prince-becomes-world-s-most-translated
-book-excluding-religious-works-1.3358885.

3. Fred Rogers, *The World According to Mister Rogers*, 179.

4. Tim Madigan, *I'm Proud of You: My Friendship with Fred Rogers* (Los Angeles: Ubuntu Press, 2012), 175; and Amy Hollingsworth, *Simple Faith of Mister Rogers*, loc. 152, Kindle.

5. Maxwell King, *The Good Neighbor: The Life and Work of Fred Rogers* (New York: Abrams, 2018), loc. 31, Kindle.

6. Fred Rogers, *Life's Journeys According to Mister Rogers*, 20.

7. King, *Good Neighbor*, loc. 39, Kindle.

8. Kiera Parrott, "You Are My Friend: The Story of Mister Rogers and His Neighborhood," *School Library Journal* 65, no. 7 (2019): 60.

9. Joanne Rogers, foreword, *The World According to Mister Rogers*, 8. Joanne discusses how her husband carried around one of his favorite quotes. A quote he loved especially—and carried around with him—was from Mary Lou Kownacki: "There isn't anyone you couldn't love once you've heard their story."

10. "Remembering Mr. Rogers (1994/1997)," 15:18.

11. "Remembering Mr. Rogers (1994/1997)."

12. John D. Barry, ed., *The Lexham Bible Dictionary* (Bellingham, WA: Lexham Press, 2016), s.v. "selah."

13. "Remembering Mr. Rogers (1994/1997)."

14. "Remembering Mr. Rogers (1994/1997)."

15. Fred Rogers, *The World According to Mister Rogers*, 179.

16. Robert Ito, "Fred Rogers' Life in 5 Artifacts," *New York Times*, June 5, 2018, https://www.nytimes.com/2018/06/05/movies/mister-rogers -wont-you-be-my-neighbor.html.

17. Jeanne Marie Laskas, as quoted in "What Is Essential Is Invisible to the Eye," in *Mister Rogers' Neighborhood: Children, Television, and Fred Rogers*, ed. M. Collins and M. M. Kimmel (Pittsburgh: University of Pittsburgh Press, 1999), 15–36.

18. Joanne Rogers, foreword, *Life's Journeys According to Mister Rogers*, 5.

19. Madigan, *I'm Proud of You*, 6.

20. Marinus H. Van Ijzendoorn, Carlo Schuengel, and Marian J. Bakermans-Kranenburg, "Disorganized Attachment in Early Childhood: Meta-Analysis of Precursors, Concomitants, and Sequelae," *Development and Psychopathology* 11, no. 2 (June 1999): 229, https://doi.org/10.1017/S09 54579499002035.

21. Knight and Sibcy, *Redeeming Attachment*, 61.

22. David H. Jonassen, *Handbook of Research on Communication and Technology*, 2nd ed. (London: Lawrence Earlbaum Associated Publishers, 2004), 297.

23. "Episode 1112," Neighborhood Archive, from *Mister Rogers' Neighborhood*, aired April 7, 1970, accessed September 19, 2019, http://www.neighborhoodarchive.com/mrn/episodes/1112/index.html; and "Fred Rogers Inducted into the TV Hall of Fame," 5:59.

24. "Mister Rogers Remixed | Garden of Your Mind | PBS Digital Studios," YouTube video, 3:13, posted by PBS Digital Studios, June 7, 2012, https://www.youtube.com/watch?v=OFzXaFbxDcM.

25. "Elie Wiesel Acceptance Speech," The Nobel Prize, from acceptance speech on December 10, 1986, in Oslo City Hall, Norway, accessed April 8, 2020, https://www.nobelprize.org/prizes/peace/1986/wiesel/acceptance-speech/.

26. James P. McCullough Jr., *Swimming Upstream: A Story about Becoming Human* (Pittsburgh: Dorrance Publishing Company, 2019).

27. Greg Kushnick, "How to Be Who You Needed as a Child," *HuffPost*, October 11, 2016, https://www.huffpost.com/entry/how-to-be-who-you-needed_b_12338116.

28. Alain Morin, "Self-Awareness Part 1: Definition, Measures, Effects, Functions, and Antecedents," *Social and Personality Psychology Compass 5*, no. 10 (2011): 808, https://onlinelibrary.wiley.com/doi/abs/10.1111/j.1751-9004.2011.00387.x.

29. Kathryn A. Oden, Janice Miner-Holden, and Richard S. Balkin, "Required Counseling for Mental Health Professional Trainees: Its Perceived Effect on Self-Awareness and Other Potential Benefits," *Journal of Mental Health* 18, no. 5 (2009): 441–48.

30. Oden, Miner-Holden, and Balkin, "Required Counseling," 441–42.

31. Colin James, "Law Student Wellbeing: Benefits of Promoting Psychological Literacy and Self-Awareness Using Mindfulness, Strengths Theory and Emotional Intelligence," *Legal Education Review* 21, nos. 1–2 (2011): 225.

32. Laskas, "What Is Essential Is Invisible to the Eye," 16.

33. Ed Yong, "The Incredible Thing We Do During Conversations," *Atlantic*, January 4, 2016, https://www.theatlantic.com/science/archive/2016/01/the-incredible-thing-we-do-during-conversations/422439/.

34. Tom Junod, "Can You Say . . . Hero?," *Esquire*, originally published November 1998, posted online April 6, 2017, https://www.esquire.com/entertainment/tv/a27134/can-you-say-hero-esq1198/.

Secret 4 Show Gratitude

1. "Fred Rogers Inducted into the TV Hall of Fame," 5:59.

2. Sara B. Algoe, Shelly L. Gable, and Natalya C. Maisel, "It's the Little Things: Everyday Gratitude as a Booster Shot for Romantic Relationships," *Personal Relationships* 17, no. 2 (2010): 217–33.

3. Robert A. Emmons and Michael E. McCullough, "Counting Blessings Versus Burdens: An Experimental Investigation of Gratitude and Subjective Well-Being in Daily Life," *Journal of Personality and Social Psychology* 84, no. 2 (2003): 377, https://psycnet.apa.org/doiLanding?doi =10.1037%2F0022-3514.84.2.377; and Martin E. P. Seligman, *Authentic Happiness: Using the New Positive Psychology to Realize Your Potential for Lasting Fulfillment* (New York: Atria, 2002), 288.

4. Michael E. McCullough et al., "Is Gratitude a Moral Affect?," *Psychological Bulletin* 127, no. 2 (2001): 249–66, https://greatergood.berkeley .edu/pdfs/GratitudePDFs/8McCullough GratitudeMoralAffect.pdf.

5. Patty Hlava and John Elfers, "The Lived Experience of Gratitude," *Journal of Humanistic Psychology* 54, no. 4 (2014): 434–55, https://www .researchgate.net/publication/258918531_The_Lived_Experience_of _Gratitude.

6. Randy A. Sansone and Lori A. Sansone, "Gratitude and Well Being: The Benefits of Appreciation," *Psychiatry (Edgmont)* 7, no. 11 (2010): 18, https://www.ncbi.nlm.nih.gov/pmc/articles/PMC3010965/.

7. Michael E. McCullough, Robert A. Emmons, and Jo-Ann Tsang, "The Grateful Disposition: A Conceptual and Empirical Topography," *Journal of Personality and Social Psychology* 82, no. 1 (2002): 113, https:// greatergood.berkeley.edu/images/application_uploads/McCullough -GratefulDisposition.pdf.

8. Seligman, *Authentic Happiness*, 288.

9. Robert A. Emmons and Robin Stern, "Gratitude as a Psychotherapeutic Intervention," *Journal of Clinical Psychology* 69, no. 8 (2013): 846, http://ei.yale.edu/wp-content/uploads/2013/11/jclp22020.pdf.

10. Emmons and Stern, "Gratitude as a Psychotherapeutic Intervention," 846; and Sansone and Sansone, "Gratitude and Well Being," 18.

11. Chih-Che Lin, "Gratitude, Positive Emotion, and Satisfaction with Life: A Test of Mediated Effect," *Social Behavior & Personality: An International Journal* 47, no. 4 (2019): 1, doi:10.2224/sbp.4398.

12. Sansone and Sansone, "Gratitude and Well Being," 18.

13. Emmons and Stern, "Gratitude as a Psychotherapeutic Intervention," 846.

14. Emmons and Stern, "Gratitude as a Psychotherapeutic Intervention," 848.

15. Sonja Lyubomirsky, *The How of Happiness: A Scientific Approach to Getting the Life You Want* (New York: Penguin Books, 2008), 22.

16. Andrea Caputo, "The Relationship between Gratitude and Loneliness: The Potential Benefits of Gratitude for Promoting Social Bonds," *Europe's Journal of Psychology* 11, no. 2 (2015): 323, https://www.ncbi .nlm.nih.gov/pmc/articles/PMC4873114/.

17. Sara B. Algoe, Jonathan Haidt, and Shelly L. Gable, "Beyond Reciprocity: Gratitude and Relationships in Everyday Life," *Emotion* 8, no. 3 (2008): 1.
18. Cameron L. Gordon, Robyn A. M. Arnette, and Rachel E. Smith, "Have You Thanked Your Spouse Today? Felt and Expressed Gratitude among Married Couples," *Personality and Individual Differences* 50, no. 3 (2011): 339–43, doi:10.1016/j.paid.2010.10.012; and Nathaniel M. Lambert and Frank D. Fincham, "Expressing Gratitude to a Partner Leads to More Relationship Maintenance Behavior," *Emotion* 11, no. 1 (2011): 1528, https://www.researchgate.net/publication/50393453_Expressing_Gratitude_to_a_Partner_Leads_to_More_Relationship_Maintenance_Behavior.
19. Anna Rotkirch et al., "Gratitude for Help among Adult Friends and Siblings," *Evolutionary Psychology* 12, no. 4 (2014): 673–86, https://journals.sagepub.com/doi/10.1177/147470491401200401.
20. Emmons and Stern, "Gratitude as a Psychotherapeutic Intervention," 849.
21. "It's Such a Good Feeling," Neighborhood Archive, song written by Fred Rogers in 1970, accessed February 19, 2020, http://www.neighborhoodarchive.com/music/songs/its_such_a_good_feeling.html.
22. Blair, "Mr Rogers' Last Goodbye before His Death Is as Heartbreaking as It Is Beautiful," Shared, April 5, 2018, https://www.shared.com/mr-rogers-farewell-message/.
23. Kirk J. Schneider, "Awakening to an Awe-Based Psychology," *Humanistic Psychologist* 39, no. 3 (2011): 247–52.
24. Harrichand, Knight, and Captari, "Impact of Emotional Intelligence," 40–47; and K. V. Petrides, "Trait Emotional Intelligence Theory," 136–39.
25. Sybil Carrere, "Welcome to the Love Lab," *Psychology Today*, September 1, 2000, https://www.psychologytoday.com/us/articles/200009/welcome-the-love-lab.
26. Alexandra Main, "Empathic Communication During Mother-Adolescent Conflict Management" (PhD diss., University of California Berkeley, 2013), http://digitalassets.lib.berkeley.edu/etd/ucb/text/Main_berkeley_0028E_13757.pdf.
27. Kimberly Lynn van Walsum, "Transference Effects on Student Physicians' Affective Interactions and Clinical Inferences in Interviews with Standardized Patients: An Experimental Study" (PhD diss., Texas A&M University, 2005), http://oaktrust.library.tamu.edu/bitstream/handle/1969.1/2548/etd-tamu-2005B-CPSY-van.pdf?sequence=1&isAllowed=y.
28. Caputo, "Relationship between Gratitude and Loneliness," 324.
29. John M. Gottman, *The Marriage Clinic: A Scientifically Based Marital Therapy* (New York: Norton, 1999), 88.
30. Thesaurus.com, s.v. "admiration," accessed September 9, 2019, https://www.thesaurus.com/browse/admiration.

31. John M. Gottman and Nan Silver, *The Seven Principles for Making Marriage Work: A Practical Guide from the Nation's Foremost Relationship Expert* (New York: Penguin, Random House, 2015), 71.

32. "Episode 1517," Neighborhood Archive, from *Mister Rogers' Neighborhood*, aired on April 26, 1983, accessed April 8, 2020, http://www.neighborhoodarchive.com/mrn/episodes/1517/index.html.

33. "Remembering Mr. Rogers (1994/1997)," 15:18.

34. Yen-Ping Chang et al., "Living with Gratitude: Spouse's Gratitude on One's Depression," *Journal of Happiness Studies* 14, no. 4 (2012): 1431–42.

35. Emmons and Stern, "Gratitude as a Psychotherapeutic Intervention," 846.

36. "Authentic Happiness," University of Pennsylvania, accessed April 8, 2020, https://www.authentichappiness.sas.upenn.edu/.

Secret 5 Develop Empathy

1. "Mister Rogers Shares an Empathetic Parenting Exercise | The Oprah Winfrey Show | OWN," YouTube video, 1:05, from *The Oprah Winfrey Show*, posted by OWN, February 20, 2018, https://www.youtube.com/watch?v=Ha7u5_L73l4.

2. "Episode 1476," Neighborhood Archive, from *Mister Rogers' Neighborhood*, aired on February 16, 1981, accessed April 8, 2020, http://www.neighborhoodarchive.com/mrn/episodes/1476/index.html.

3. Fred Rogers, *Dear Mister Rogers: Does It Ever Rain in Your Neighborhood?* (New York: Penguin Books, 1996), 38.

4. Christine Teigen (@chrissyteigen), Twitter post, February 19, 2018, 8:23 p.m., https://twitter.com/chrissyteigen/status/965758687414554624?lang=en.

5. Ann C. Rumble, Paul A. M. Van Lange, and Craig D. Parks, "The Benefits of Empathy: When Empathy May Sustain Cooperation in Social Dilemmas," *European Journal of Social Psychology* 40, no. 5 (2010): 856–66, https://www.researchgate.net/publication/227746962_The_Benefits_of_Empathy_When_Empathy_May_Sustain_Cooperation_in_Social_Dilemmas.

6. Michele Borba, "The Many Benefits of Empathy and Why It Matters for Kids in a 'Me-First' World," *Work & Family Life* 31, no. 9 (2016): 1.

7. Borba, "Many Benefits of Empathy," 1.

8. Björn N. Persson et al., "Empathy and Universal Values Explicated by the Empathy-Altruism Hypothesis," *Journal of Social Psychology* 156, no. 6 (2016): 610–19.

9. Christopher D. Schmidt and Nathan C. Gehlert, "Couples Therapy and Empathy: An Evaluation of the Impact of Imago Relationship Therapy on Partner Empathy Levels," *Family Journal* 25, no. 1 (2017): 23–30.

10. Schmidt and Gehlert, "Couples Therapy and Empathy," 23.

11. Jolien Van der Graaff et al., "The Moderating Role of Empathy in the Association between Parental Support and Adolescent Aggressive and Delinquent Behavior," *Aggressive Behavior* 38, no. 5 (2012): 368.

12. Jan-Louw Kotze and Lisa A. Turner, "Parental Warmth and Interpersonal Empathy as Predictors of Sexual Assault Bystander Intervention Efficacy," *Journal of Interpersonal Violence* (2019), https://www.ncbi.nlm.nih.gov/pubmed/30975022.

13. Alexander Soutschek and Philippe Tobler, "Motivation for the Greater Good: Neural Mechanisms of Overcoming Costs," *Current Opinion in Behavioral Sciences* 22 (2018): 96–105, doi:10.1016/j.cobeha.2018.01.025; and Cell Press, "Brain Imaging Reveals Neural Roots of Caring." ScienceDaily, June 8, 2017, www.sciencedaily.com/releases/2017/06/170608123653.htm.

14. Chris Voss, *Never Split the Difference: Negotiating as If Your Life Depended on It* (New York: HarperCollins, 2016), 54.

15. Kristin D. Neff, "Self-Compassion: An Alternative Conceptualization of a Healthy Attitude toward Oneself," *Self and Identity* 2 (2003): 87.

16. Neff, "Self-Compassion," 62, 86, 182, 201; and Byron Brown, *Soul without Shame: A Guide to Liberating Yourself from the Judge Within* (Boston: Shambala, 1999), 302.

17. Borba, "Many Benefits of Empathy," 1.

18. "Empathy? In Denmark They're Learning It in School," *Morning Future*, April 26, 2019, https://www.morningfuture.com/en/article/2019/04/26/empathy-happiness-school-denmark/601/.

19. John F. Helliwell, Richard Layard, and Jeffrey D. Sachs, "World Happiness Report 2019," New York: Sustainable Development Solutions Network, accessed April 8, 2020, https://s3.amazonaws.com/happiness-report/2019/WHR19.pdf.

20. "Empathy?" *Morning Future.*

21. "Empathy?" *Morning Future.*

22. Jessica Joelle Alexander and Iben Sandahl, *The Danish Way of Parenting: What the Happiest People in the World Know about Raising Confident, Capable Kids* (New York: Tarcher Perigree, 2016), 86.

23. Meik Wiking, *The Little Book of Hygge: Danish Secrets to Happy Living* (New York: William Morrow, 2017), loc. 256, Kindle.

24. Wiking, *Little Book of Hygge*, loc. 4, Kindle.

Secret 6 Practice Acceptance

1. "Fred Rogers on Television's Responsibility to Children," interview by Karen Herman, Television Academy Foundation, July 22, 1999, https://interviews.televisionacademy.com/interviews/fred-rogers.

2. Albert Ellis, "How to Fix the Empty Self," *American Psychologist* 46, no. 5 (1991), 539, https://psycnet.apa.org/fulltext/1991-28120-001.pdf

3. Douglas K. MacInnes, "Self-Esteem and Self-Acceptance: An Examination into Their Relationship and Their Effect on Psychological Health," *Journal of Psychiatric and Mental Health Nursing* 13, no. 5 (2006): 483–89, doi:10.1111/j.1365–2850.2006.00959.x.

4. Hedda Sharapan, personal communication from July 31, 2013, as quoted in Jeana Lietz, "Journey to the Neighborhood: An Analysis of Fred Rogers and His Lessons for Educational Leaders," Loyola University Chicago, 2014, https://ecommons.luc.edu/cgi/viewcontent.cgi?article=2096 &context=luc_diss, 121.

5. "Mister Rogers Draws a House," YouTube video, 0:17, from *Mister Rogers' Neighborhood*, posted by Fred McFeely Rogers, November 12, 2019, https://www.youtube.com/watch?v=tEmjec3yBFc.

6. "Fred Rogers' 2002 Dartmouth College Commencement Address," YouTube video, 13:16, posted by Dartmouth, March 27, 2018, https://www.youtube.com/watch?v=907yEkALaAY.

7. William Damon, *Greater Expectations: Overcoming the Culture of Indulgence in America's Homes and Schools* (New York: Free Press, 1995), 58, 77.

8. Danilo Garcia, Ali Al Nima, and Oscar N. E. Kjell, "The Affective Profiles, Psychological Well-Being, and Harmony: Environmental Mastery and Self-Acceptance Predict the Sense of a Harmonious Life," *PeerJ* 2 (2014), https://peerj.com/articles/259/.

9. Shelley H. Carson and Ellen J. Langer, "Mindfulness and Self-Acceptance," *Journal of Rational-Emotive & Cognitive-Behavior Therapy* 24, no. 1 (Spring 2006): 39, https://www.researchgate.net/publication/226501882_Mindfulness_and_self-acceptance.

10. Kristin D. Neff, Kristin L. Kirkpatrick, and Stephanie S. Rudea, "Self-Compassion and Adaptive Psychological Functioning," *Journal of Research in Personality* 41, no. 1 (2007): 139–54, https://self-compassion.org/wp-content/uploads/publications/JRP.pdf.

11. Sherlyn S. Jimenezab, Barbara L. Nilesb, and Crystal L. Parka, "A Mindfulness Model of Affect Regulation and Depressive Symptoms: Positive Emotions, Mood Regulation Expectancies, and Self-Acceptance as Regulatory Mechanisms," *Personality and Individual Differences* 49, no. 6 (2010): 646.

12. Jimenezab, Nilesb, and Parka, "Mindfulness Model," 646; and Gordon L. Flett et al., "Dimensions of Perfectionism, Unconditional Self-Acceptance, and Depression," *Journal of Rational-Emotive and Cognitive-Behavior Therapy* 21 (2003): 119–38; and Garcia, Nima, and Kjell, "Affective Profiles."

13. Omri Gillath, Phillip R. Shaver, and Mario Mikulincer, "An Attachment-Theoretical Approach to Compassion and Altruism," in

Compassion: Conceptualisations, Research, and Use in Psychotherapy, ed. Paul Gilbert (New York: Routledge, 2005), 140.

14. Jude Cassidy, "The Nature of a Child's Ties," in Jude Cassidy and Phillip Shaver, *The Handbook of Attachment: Theory, Research and Clinical Applications* (New York: Guilford Press), 3.

15. Abraham Maslow, *Maslow on Management* (New York: John Wiley, 1998), xx.

16. Carl R. Rogers, *A Way of Being* (New York: Houghton Mifflin, 1980), 22.

17. Carl R. Rogers, *On Becoming a Person: A Therapist's View of Psychotherapy* (New York: Houghton Mifflin, 1961), 32.

18. Clinton and Sibcy, *Attachments*, 263.

19. Carl R. Rogers, *On Becoming a Person*, 21.

Secret 7 Establish Security

1. Andrew Coleman, *Dictionary of Psychology*, 2nd ed. (Oxford: Oxford University Press, 2006), 688.

2. Leigh Blickley, "The Gay 'Ghetto Boy' Who Bonded with Mister Rogers and Changed the Neighborhood," *HuffPost*, June 8, 2018, https://www.huffpost.com/entry/mister-rogers-francois-clemmons_n_5b15a5b 6e4b014707d275904.

3. Sally I. Maximo and Jennifer S. Carranza, "Parental Attachment and Love Language as Determinants of Resilience among Graduating University Students," *SAGE Open* 6, no. 1 (2016): 3, https://journals.sage pub.com/doi/pdf/10.1177/2158244015622800; and Deborah Tannen, *You Just Don't Understand: Women and Men in Conversation* (New York: Harper Collins, 1990), 46.

4. Maximo and Carranza, "Parental Attachment and Love Language," 1.

5. John Bowlby, *Attachment and Loss*, vol.1 (New York: Basic Books, 1973), 316.

6. James Coan, "Toward a Neuroscience of Attachment," in *Handbook of Attachment: Theory, Research, and Clinical Implications*, 2nd ed., ed. Jude Cassidy and Philip R. Shaver (New York: Guilford Press, 2008), 13, https://www.researchgate.net/profile/James_Coan/publication /230669685_Toward_a_Neuroscience_of_Attachment/links/0fcfd502d3 9a581d8e000000.pdf; and Harrichand, Knight, and Captari, "The Impact of Emotional Intelligence," 40–47.

7. Knight and Sibcy, *Redeeming Attachment*, 25.

8. "Remembering Mr. Rogers (1994/1997)," 15:18.

9. "Koko the Gorilla Meets Mister Rogers, Her Favorite Celebrity," YouTube video, 0:46, Mister Rogers met Koko on May 18, 1999, posted

by kokoflix, August 3, 2009, https://www.youtube.com/watch?v=cn79 Lgfh1hw.

10. The story of the young boy with cerebral palsy can be found at Tom Junod, "Can You Say . . . Hero?"

11. John Kuhnley, *The Female Brain* (Dubuque, IA: Kendall Hunt, forthcoming).

12. "Carl Rogers & Gloria Counselling – Part 1," YouTube video, tape of a counseling session between Carl Rogers and Gloria, posted by esherborne3, November 27, 2008, https://www.youtube.com /watch?v=ZBkUqcqRChg&list=PLFC8B8CE02600F962&index=5.

13. Peter Fonagy, Howard Steele, and Miriam Steele, "Maternal Representations of Attachment during Pregnancy Predict the Organization of Infant-Mother Attachment at One Year of Age," *Child Development* 62, no. 5 (1991): 891–905.

14. Pat Brady and Don Wimmer, "Rose Is Rose," GoComics, January 21, 2002, https://www.gocomics.com/roseisrose/2002/01/21.

15. Brady and Wimmer, "Rose Is Rose."

16. Lee A. Kirkpatrick, "God as a Substitute Attachment Figure: A Longitudinal Study of Adult Attachment Style and Religious Change in College Students," *Personality and Social Psychology Bulletin* 24, no. 9 (1998): 961–73, https://journals.sagepub.com/doi/10.1177/0146167298249004.

17. O. Gillath, E. Selcuk, and P. R. Shaver, "Moving toward a Secure Attachment Style: Can Repeated Security Priming Help?," *Social & Personality Psychology Compass* 2 (2008): 1651–66, https://www.research gate.net/publication/227520134_Moving_Toward_a_Secure_Attach ment_Style_Can_Repeated_Security_Priming_Help.

18. Clinton and Sibcy, *Attachments*, 21–33, 179.

19. Knight and Sibcy, *Redeeming Attachment*, 23.

20. Carl R. Rogers, *On Becoming a Person*, 283.

Closing Thoughts: Does Mister Rogers Still Live in Your Neighborhood?

1. Brené Brown, *Daring Greatly: How the Courage to Be Vulnerable Transforms the Way We Live, Love, Parent, and Lead* (New York: Avery, 2012), loc. 1749, Kindle.

2. Fred Rogers, *The World According to Mister Rogers*, 220.

3. Fred Rogers, *The World According to Mister Rogers*, loc. 560, Kindle.

Anita Knight Kuhnley, PhD, has trained counselors at Liberty University for the past decade and now serves at her alma mater as an associate professor of counseling in the School of Psychology and Counseling at Regent University in Virginia Beach, VA. She teaches in the CACREP-accredited counseling program. Kuhnley also trains developing counselors and enjoys journeying with students in the exploration of counseling research and the process of becoming. She has always loved Mister Rogers and aims to bring the "Mister Rogers Effect" to each of her classes. Kuhnley earned her doctorate in counselor education and supervision and her MA in community counseling from Regent University. She is also certified as a highly reliable coder of the Adult Attachment Interview (AAI) through Mary Main and Eric Hesse's UC Berkeley AAI coder certification program. With her husband and their two poodle pups, she lives in Lynchburg, Virginia, and loves to adventure anywhere she can see the deep blue sea. Kuhnley is also the author of several books, including *Redeeming Attachment*, *Counseling Women*, and *Research-Based Counseling Skills*. For more information, visit her website at dranitakuhnley.com.

Connect with
Anita

To learn more about Anita's research and
books, or to contact her, head to

dranitakuhnley.com

 AnitaKuhnley

 The.Empathetic.Counselor

Connect with
BakerBooks
Relevant. Intelligent. Engaging.

Sign up for announcements about
new and upcoming titles at

BakerBooks.com/SignUp

@ReadBakerBooks

"In books we have the richest **treasures** on earth."

—HERMAN BAKER, 1911–1991

COME VISIT US AT

2768 East Paris Ave. SE
Grand Rapids, MI 49546

Or shop online at
BAKERBOOKHOUSE.COM

Any questions? Give us a call at (616) 957-3110.